Read-Aloud Plays

Ancient Egypt

by John Rearick

SCHOLASTIC
PROFESSIONAL BOOKS

NEW YORK   TORONTO   LONDON   AUCKLAND   SYDNEY
MEXICO CITY   NEW DELHI   HONG KONG   BUENOS AIRES

FOR MY FAMILY

Cover and interior design by Josué Castilleja
Cover and interior illustrations by Mona Mark

ISBN 0-590-64404-1

CONTENTS

INTRODUCTION

WHY STUDY ANCIENT EGYPT?

If you are ever looking for a reason to study Egypt as part of a curriculum on the ancient world, you need only to look at a map. For thousands of years Egypt has stood at the heart of several critically important civilizations. To the north of ancient Egypt was the Mediterranean world of the Greeks and the Romans. To the south of the Egyptian pyramids, the continent of Africa, with its myriad peoples and cultures, stretched on and on. To the east, there were the Sumerians, the Hittites, and the Babylonians. Egypt influenced and, in turn, was influenced by these other societies, at times subtly and at times directly. To study the ancient world without studying Egypt would be like building a wheel without a hub or spokes.

In addition to being of central importance, ancient Egypt is a fascinating subject that will captivate your students. Some aspects of Egyptian civilization seem very familiar to us, and some are so commonplace that they are almost invisible. You might want to point out to students, for instance, that most Americans routinely carry a picture of a pyramid in their wallets, on the one-dollar bill. But other aspects of the ancient society seem very foreign. The Egyptian gods seems much more exotic than their Greek counterparts. The deep fascination the Egyptians had for the afterlife is both mysterious and spellbinding for us, centuries and centuries after the impressive pyramids of Giza were erected and the fascinating tombs of the Valley of the Kings, across the Nile from present-day Luxor, were hewn from rock, painstakingly detailed, and then sealed.

Strangely enough, the study of ancient Egypt is also a relatively new field, and students should be reminded that they are young researchers. Students of Greek mythology were already studying Homer's *Iliad* and *Odyssey* in 400 B.C. Though Greek and Roman writers recorded their impressions of Egypt in ancient times, many of the secrets of Egypt were locked away, coded in hieroglyphics on the walls of tombs. While there was a renaissance of Greek and Roman thought from in the fourteenth through the seventeenth centuries, Egypt remained behind an impenetrable veil. The discovery of the Rosetta Stone in 1799 led to the eventual breaking of the hieroglyphic code. This means that much of the information about Egypt is "newer" than the primary sources relating to the American Revolution.

Aside from its historical value, Egypt has given us great stories, and this may be the most compelling reason to expose students to this culture. The plays included in this volume are based on a variety of stories: common folk tales, priestly myths, and historical records. With luck, these plays will provide a taste of some of the characters and plots that existed in ancient Egypt, and your students will be intrigued enough to do even more research on their own.

For many of us, the word *Egyptian* may conjure up images of endless lines of tomb paintings depicting two-dimensional people and animals, all standing in what appear to be rather uncomfortable positions. But in my research, I came to see the ancient Egyptians as anything but stiff, flat characters. Their love of stories and the joy that they found in life were astounding. Perhaps one of the reasons that they were so preoccupied with the afterlife is that they thoroughly cherished this life.

KEY CONCEPTS

As you embark on your study of Egypt, here are some of the topics that you will no doubt encounter. Use this list as a quick reference guide. For in-depth explanations, please refer to the books in the Additional Resources section at the end of this book.

PYRAMIDS

When most people think of the pyramids of Egypt, they are imagining the three pyramids located neer Giza (*GEE za*), a short distance outside the modern city of Cairo. (Nearby, they are guarded by the Great Sphinx—an image of a pharaoh as part human, part lion.) These amazing structures were built during what is known as the Fourth Dynasty (about 2613 to 2494 B.C.). They served as tombs with platforms for special rites for the dead and may have been designed to symbolize the slanting rays of the sun. They each contain underground passageways, ceremonial rooms, and a burial chamber. The Great Pyramid of Kufu, the largest, covers about 13 acres at its base and consists of about 2,300,000 blocks of stone. It probably took about 20 years to build. Although tradition associates the pyramids with slave labor, many historians believe that the monuments were, in fact, vast public works projects, built with public tax money and employing thousands of laborers.

PHARAOH

The word *pharaoh* is derived from the word for the royal house, but it eventually came to refer to the ruler, as well as the palace in which he lived. The pharaoh was considered to be the living embodiment of the god Horus and, as leader, had a crucial religious and political role in society. (For more background on this point, read the play in this book devoted to the myth of Isis and Osiris.) Usually the kings named their direct descendants to be their successors, though this wasn't always the case. (See the story of Hatshepsut for one of these exceptions.)

THE NILE, THE RIVER OF LIFE

Egypt is a large country on the North African shore of the Mediterranean Sea, but a quick glimpse at the map can be deceptive. Much of Egypt is made up of uninhabitable desert. The Nile River, which flows north from sources in central Africa, brings life into the land. Crops and, by extension, all life in ancient Egypt depended upon a yearly event: the inundation, or flooding, of the Nile. When the river rose over its banks, it irrigated the desert and created very fertile farmland. In time, the Egyptians learned to preserve the overflowing waters to use for irrigation. The Nile was also an important source of transportation. It connected Upper Egypt, which was in south, with Lower Egypt, which was in the north and contained the Nile delta. One measure of how important the Nile was is that model ships are often found among the artifacts buried with influential people.

MUMMIES

When the prehistoric people in Egypt buried their dead in the sands on the fringes of their settlements, they noticed that the climate dried and preserved the remains of the deceased. This natural phenomenon was developed into an elaborate process as Egyptian civilization evolved. Using a variety of natural substances, including a salt-like substance called *natron*, and some sophisticated but gruesome surgical techniques, priests in charge of burial would remove the internal organs of the deceased and pack the corpses with drying agents. The internal organs were placed in vessels known as *canopic jars*. The body was then wrapped in many layers of linen. Sometimes the wrapping itself could take weeks. Depending on the rank and

affluence of the deceased, the body was then covered with jewels, masks, and possibly placed in a coffin in the shape of a human body. The entire pre-burial process was said to take 70 days. Poorer Egyptians could afford only a much simpler version of this process. The mummification procedure was thought to be overseen by Anubis, the jackal-headed god of embalming.

HIEROGLYPHICS

The Egyptians revered writing and believed that it was an invention of the god Thoth. Writing underwent several stages of development in Egypt. It seems that at first, in the system known as hieroglyphics, Egyptians used a picture to approximate the sound of a syllable. In some cases, however, rather than compose a long list of pictures—say, four or five—to show the sounds of the syllables of a simple word, it was easier just to include a picture of the thing itself. (It was more efficient to draw a house than to sound out the word for it.) Later, scribes began to employ a cursive script called

hieratic from a word meaning "priestly" for everyday business. This script was abbreviated even more under a shorthand system known as *demotic* from a word meaning "popular."

GODS

The ancient Egyptians were generally polytheistic and the Egyptian gods are a complicated group. While the story of Isis and Osiris (see the play in this volume for the full story) is an important centerpiece for understanding Egyptian gods, there is no official list or hierarchy of them. There was apparently a wide variety of gods, and at different times one god gained dominance over another. The god Amun was a deity whose followers were concentrated around the city of Thebes in Upper Egypt. When Thebes became a powerful city, Amun became a very important god throughout Egypt. Over time, gods acquired new attributes or characteristics, so that, depending on the age of the source, the same gods may have slightly different identities.

Here are some of the gods who appear most frequently in art and in mythology:

- Amun, *(AH mun)* also called Amon: the creator god
- Re, also called Ra: the god of the sun
- Geb: the god of the earth
- Isis: *(EYE sis)* the goddess of the moon, who established marriage and helped civilize Egypt
- Osiris: *(o SIRE us)* the god of the afterlife, who was once a king on earth who civlized Egypt
- Horus: the god of light, order, and kingship, who appears with the head of a hawk
- Nut: the goddess of the sky
- Hathor: the goddess of love
- Anubis: *(a NU bis)* the god of embalming, with the head of a jackal
- Nepthys: *(NEP this)* the goddess of death
- Set, also called Seth: the god of darkness and chaos
- Thoth: the god of wisdom, depicted with the head of an ibis, a long-billed wading bird

 # THE TOMB THIEF

CHARACTERS

- Narrator, Dadat looking back from his old age
- Pharaoh, the king of Egypt
- Dadat, the young Prime Minister of ancient Egypt
- Builder, the architect of the tomb
- Sety, the son of the builder, the brother of Pepy
- Pepy, the son of the builder, the brother of Sety
- Mother, the mother of Sety and Pepy
- Guard
- Princess, the daughter of the Pharaoh

BACKGROUND

When asked about Egypt, the first things that many people think of are the pyramids. The pyramids of Egypt are spectacular today, but imagine how amazing they must have been in the eyes of people who lived in the ancient world. The Great Pyramid, which was built around 2500 B.C., covers about 13 acres at its base. It is made of limestone blocks, each weighing about two and a half tons. Thousands of Egyptians worked on this tomb, many probably during the yearly season when the Nile flooded their land and they couldn't farm.

Why did the Egyptians spend so much time and energy building a tomb for their leader? In ancient Egypt, the pharaoh was considered a god and the great link between humans and the rest of the gods. If he had a successful afterlife, it meant that they, too, were likely to have a happy eternal life. There was also a very down-to-earth reason. The workers probably received payment—perhaps in food or money—which would have helped them until their crops were harvested.

The Egyptians were ingenious engineers who figured out how to move gigantic stones thousands of years before there were construction cranes and steam shovels. No doubt, however, some Egyptians were experts of a different sort. Every era has its thieves. What could be more challenging than figuring out how to break into the pharaoh's tomb?

This story is based on a tale recorded by the Greek historian Herodotus (he ROD a tus) who visited Egypt in ancient times.

SCENE ONE

NARRATOR: I am retired now, but in my day I was the right-hand man of the Pharaoh, a great leader and powerful man. I'm tired now, and I don't care to discuss the "good old days." However, I'll never forget the story of the treasure thieves and what my master, the Pharaoh, did about them. (*closing his eyes to remember the distant past*) I can still remember how it all started, as many things then did, with my master yelling . . .

PHARAOH: (*shouting*) Minister, where are you? Why aren't you ever here when I need you?

DADAT: I'm sorry, Your Highness, but I was dealing with a report of famine in Lower Egypt. Remember how you told me to make it my top priority yesterday?

PHARAOH: Yes, I vaguely remember, but that will have to wait now. Something else has come up that needs your immediate and undivided attention. Make *this* your top priority!

DADAT: Sir, I'll do my best.

PHARAOH: You had better. Now, listen. I've made two important discoveries.

DADAT: Is there corruption in the government, Your Highness? Did the other gods share some new information with you? Is the Nile about to flood?

PHARAOH: No, nothing like that. I discovered two very important things about myself. First, I realized that I am growing old. Second, I realized that I am too rich. What do you propose to do about these serious problems?

DADAT: Your Highness, everyone gets old, and I've never heard a person complain about being too rich. Besides, you've always been rather stingy . . . I mean, careful . . . with your money. Do you recall when we spoke about my salary that time?

PHARAOH: How dare you speak to me in such a fashion! Call the guards and have yourself arrested and executed.

DADAT: Wait, Your Highness. Let's not overreact. I just realized how serious your problems really are. Remember that it takes the human brain a while to catch up with your godlike thinking.

PHARAOH: Well, I suppose you are right.

DADAT: Also, I think I have a solution to your problems.

PHARAOH: You'd better speak quickly, or I'll call the guards myself.

DADAT: It's time to build a tomb, one that will be an everlasting monument to your power and that can hold some of your wealth for the afterlife. You should build your tomb, just as your father and grandfather built theirs.

PHARAOH: An excellent idea! Build one immediately.

DADAT: Whatever you say, I will obey.

PHARAOH: Start construction right away.

DADAT: Yes, Your Highness.

PHARAOH: I don't want to wait until I'm dead to enjoy my tomb.

DADAT: Splendid idea, Your Highness.

PHARAOH: Oh, there is one more thing.

DADAT: Yes, Your Highness?

PHARAOH: I don't want this to cost an arm and a leg.

DADAT: But you said you were too rich.

PHARAOH: Don't be ridiculous. Who can be too rich?

SCENE TWO

NARRATOR: (*with his eyes open now*) With my life at stake, I did what I had to do. I hired the best tomb builder in Egypt. At least, he was the best builder available. Everyone else seems to have been busy.

BUILDER: I am so honored that you have chosen me, Prime Minister, to serve the Pharaoh. Serving him will be a reward all by itself.

DADAT: I am glad you feel that way, because there is a slight problem you are going to have to deal with.

BUILDER: Don't worry! I am experienced and I come from a long line of builders. My great-grandfather worked on the pyramids of Giza! My father carved stone for the Temple of Karnak! What's the problem? Shifting sands at the building site? Bad stone from the quarry? Lazy workers?

DADAT: No, I'm afraid it's none of those things. It's money.

BUILDER: Money! Always an issue! I'll try to keep the costs down as much as possible.

DADAT: No, you don't understand. There is plenty of money for the building. The Pharaoh wants it to look great. The problem is that the Pharaoh doesn't want to pay you much. He's a bit of a miser, to put it bluntly.

BUILDER: Well, money is rather important to me, now that you mention it. Suppose we call this whole thing off. I think I've got some other work to do and . . .

DADAT: I'm afraid that is impossible. You've been selected for this royal task. Abandoning your job now might be considered an act of treason. You know what the punishment for treason is, don't you?

BUILDER: Bad seats for next year's Nile floods?

DADAT: No, death.

BUILDER: I see. Then I should build this great tomb for the glory of the Pharaoh and be grateful for anything I get.

DADAT: Builder, you seem to be getting smarter and smarter. I like a person who learns on the job.

NARRATOR: And so the builder set to work. He wasn't happy about the job, but he worked hard at it. It took many years, and the builder became an old man, as I did, but the tomb was finally completed. I remember when I took the Pharaoh to see it.

PHARAOH: Marvelous! Terrific! The builder has done a splendid job! Double the bonus! I did offer the builder a bonus, didn't I?

DADAT: Yes, Your Majesty. I'll see that he receives four loaves of bread. I'm sure that he'll be most appreciative, especially since I hear he's close to death.

PHARAOH: I may be being too generous, but I can't help myself. Make it day-old bread. Now, arrange for the first truckload of gold and jewels to be brought into my tomb.

NARRATOR: I didn't know at the time that the builder was arranging for his own little bonus. He had called his two sons, Sety and Pepy, to see him.

BUILDER: Come close and listen to me, boys. You know that I gave the best years of my life to that Pharaoh, and he never paid me a decent salary. Now I am going to die without having wealth to pass on to you. You and your mother will be very poor.

SETY: Don't worry, Father. We'll survive somehow. After all, we've learned to eat very little.

BUILDER: Listen to what I say and you'll never have to worry about being hungry again. When I built the tomb, I created a secret passageway inside it. On the east side, the fifth stone from the edge will slide aside if you push it. You'll see a long, narrow passageway, just big enough for a person to crawl through. That tunnel will lead you right to the treasure room!

SETY: Father, we're too honest to steal from the Pharaoh. Besides, he might need to have all that gold and all those priceless jewels for his life after death. Perhaps we should just beg for bread.

PEPY: Are you crazy? We deserve some of that treasure! Dad worked his heart out on that project. Let's go to the tomb tonight!

BUILDER: No, wait, boys. Spend the time I have remaining with me. Besides, give the Pharaoh time to fill the place with treasure. Then you can have your pick of the greatest riches in the world!

SCENE THREE

NARRATOR: The builder's sons waited. They watched each day as carefully guarded, covered carts rolled up to the tomb's entrance. They cried and mourned when their father's spirit passed out of this world and into the afterlife. Finally, they could stay away no longer. One night they sneaked up to the tomb.

SETY: *(whispering)* Pepy, here is the fifth stone. Look how easily it moves aside when you press it!

PEPY: Hey, there is the tunnel that Father told us about. Bring the torch inside!

NARRATOR: They crawled through the long, dark tunnel to the treasure chamber. When they stepped into the treasure chamber, they were stunned.

PEPY: Look at the wealth! All the glimmering gold hurts my eyes.

SETY: So do the shining jewels.

PEPY: Father, I know you can hear us. You really did make us rich men! Thank you!

SETY: Let's help ourselves to that pile of gold rings first.

NARRATOR: They lost no time in filling their bags with stolen treasure.

PEPY: *(breathing heavily under the strain)* My loot bag is already almost too heavy to carry.

SETY: Father, why didn't you make this passageway a bit wider? We need a cart to carry out the treasure.

NARRATOR: When the brothers had taken as much as they could carry, they crawled back through the tunnel and replaced the sliding stone. The next day the Pharaoh went to the tomb to visit his treasure.

PHARAOH: I have to be the richest man in history. Look at the jewels, look at the gold rings! Hey, wait a minute. That pile looks quite a bit shorter than it did yesterday. Prime Minister! What's been going on here?

DADAT: Your Highness, you yourself sealed this tomb when you left yesterday. No one could have entered!

PHARAOH: No one! You'd better be right. I'm going to count the rings this time, just to make sure. Sit down, Prime Minister. This is going to take some time!

NARRATOR: That night, shortly after the Pharaoh had finished counting his gold, the brothers revisited the tomb and walked off with more of the King's gold. When the Pharaoh returned to the tomb and discovered that the gold was gone, he hit the cornice!

PHARAOH: What's going on here? The tomb's been sealed, but someone's been stealing my gold. It's as if they manage to pass right though the walls!

DADAT: Perhaps it is a ghost, Your Highness.

PHARAOH: It must be a greedy ghost! No, I smell a treacherous human in this. Here's what we should do. Place traps all around the floor in the treasure chamber. Make sure the traps are not obvious. We'll catch those ghosts if they try to steal again.

NARRATOR: Sety and Pepy returned again that night, hungry for more gold. In their eagerness for more loot, they did not see the traps that the Pharaoh had set for them.

PEPY: Ahhh! Something just bit me! No, my leg is caught in a trap. I can't get it out!

SETY: *(straining to open the trap)* Sorry, brother, but you're stuck! We'll have to wait until the guards find us.

PEPY: Both of us will be executed!

SETY: No, you're wrong. We'll probably be tortured first, then executed.

PEPY: Brother, listen. Escape with your life and return home to our mother. Take care of her and use the gold we've got.

SETY: I can't do that! I can't just leave you here to be arrested!

PEPY: You must or our whole family will be lost. There is also one more thing you must do to prevent the Pharaoh from discovering my identity. Will you promise?

SETY: Of course I promise. What is that?

PEPY: You must cut off my head with your sword so that no one will be able to identify my body. Remember, I'm older and you must listen to me!

SETY: No . . . no . . .

PEPY: A promise is a promise.

NARRATOR: The younger brother did as he was told, and the next day the Pharaoh opened the sealed tomb and found inside it a headless corpse. He wasn't pleased.

PHARAOH: The thieves have escaped me—well, all except this one. I'll question the prisoner and find his identity. His entire family will pay for this insult!

DADAT: Ah, Your Highness, you might find it difficult to get a straight answer out of the prisoner. Did you notice that his head was missing?

PHARAOH: (*becoming more angry*) Don't bother me with details! (*shouting*) Guards, take this body and hang it from the palace walls. If anyone sees the body and starts to act upset, arrest that person immediately! We will find this thief's family yet!

SCENE FOUR

NARRATOR: Naturally, the mother of the surviving thief was terribly upset about her son's death.

MOTHER: I can't even give my child's body a decent burial. What will happen to him in the afterlife?

SETY: Mother, please calm down.

MOTHER: We've got to do something. Unless we get your brother's body back, I'm going to the Pharaoh myself to confess.

SETY: Wait, Mom! Don't do anything rash. We would all end up hanging from the palace wall.

MOTHER: At least we'd all be together!

SETY: I've got a plan that might work!

NARRATOR: So Sety put his plan into action. First, he used some of the gold to buy some donkeys. On these donkeys he put skins full of the most expensive wine he could find. Then he drove the donkeys to the wall of the palace, where the guards were watching over his brother's body.

SETY: I'll just take out the stoppers from a few of these wineskins and see what happens.

GUARD: You there, what are you up to? Move along there, unless you know who this thief is.

SETY: Help! Oh, help! The delicious, expensive wine I've been carrying is leaking out. Help! Are there any brave soldiers in the area?

GUARD: We'd be more than glad to help! (*shouting to the other guards*) Come on, boys, we've finally got a job that suits us!

NARRATOR: The guards grabbed whatever they could—cups, bowls, and even their helmets. They ran to the wineskins and caught as much wine as they could. And they drank it!

SETY: Hey, you said you were going to help me, not steal my wine.

GUARD: Take it easy, stranger. We soldiers deserve a break once in a while. Besides, you've got plenty of wine left. By the way, this wine is delicious!

SETY: Thanks for the compliment, Officer. I'm sorry that I was ungrateful to you and your men. I suppose I should be more generous with our boys in uniform. Why don't you and your men be my guests and allow me to pour you some more wine?

NARRATOR: One sip of wine led to another. Soon the soldiers had finished all the wine that Sety had brought. Under the influence of the drink, they became very sleepy. One by one, they nodded off.

GUARD: I'm sure that no one would mind if we took a little nap here in the shade. After all, that dead man is not going to run away! Ha!

SETY: Now, I'll take back my brother's body so that we can give it a decent burial. I'll also leave a calling card so that the soldiers will remember me for a little while.

NARRATOR: After he had loaded the body onto the donkey, he shaved the right cheek of each of the sleeping soldiers. The Pharaoh had no trouble identifying the soldiers who had let him down.

PHARAOH: Bring me those half-bearded excuses for soldiers! Let's see how close a sword can shave!

SCENE FIVE

NARRATOR: By this point, the Pharaoh was really mad. He thought that the thief must be laughing at him, so he made the thief's capture his top priority, more important than wars or other affairs of state.

PHARAOH: I'll show this thief who's the most cunning person in Egypt! Where's my daughter?

PRINCESS: Right here, Father.

PHARAOH: I'm going to set another trap for this clever fellow. I'll send out a proclamation announcing that it's time you were married. Anyone in the kingdom may be eligible to marry you.

PRINCESS: Father, you said that I could marry a rich prince. I don't like common people!

PHARAOH: *(becoming frustrated)* This is just a trap. Listen. Whoever wants to marry you will have to tell you the wickedest and cleverest thing he's ever done. You'll agree to marry the one with the best story.

PRINCESS: *(beginning to whine)* I want to marry a prince. You said I could.

PHARAOH: Don't be silly. You will marry a rich man, someone who will make me lots of money. You'll just pretend that you'll marry the man with the best stories. When you hear someone tell you about stealing from my tomb, grab him and call for the guards. We'll have our thief.

NARRATOR: The announcement went out across the kingdom. Young men began to line up to tell the Princess their stories of cleverness and wickedness. Sety couldn't resist the challenge.

SETY: I know this is a trap, but I also know I can outsmart the Pharaoh. I'll see the Princess, but first I'll stop by the morticians.

MOTHER: Oh, my son, are you going to make your funeral arrangements in advance?

SETY: No, Mother, I've got another plan in mind.

NARRATOR: Using his tricks, Sety managed somehow to get a dead man's arm. He placed this arm under his cloak so that it looked like his own. Then he went to see the Princess. Sety waited in a long line, and, finally, he was escorted in to see the Princess.

PRINCESS: *(sounding bored)* Next! What is it? It had better be good. *(to herself)* None of the men in this kingdom has done anything clever or wicked! I behaved worse before I was seven years old.

SETY: Oh, Princess, I've done something terrible.

PRINCESS: That's what they all say.

SETY: No, really. I am a wanted man.

PRINCESS: *(interested)* Really? Do tell!

SETY: I had to cut off my brother's head when he was caught in a trap in the Pharaoh's treasure room!

PRINCESS: *(grabbing Sety's false arm)* Fascinating! Now, tell me, did you do anything clever?

SETY: Yes. I tricked the palace guards and stole his body back!

PRINCESS: Guards! Guards! Arrest this man!

NARRATOR: Though the Princess thought she had a firm grip on Sety, he jumped up and ran out through the doors before the guards could arrest him. She was left holding the arm.

PRINCESS: Yuckkkk! That's the last time I do a favor for my father. I hate to admit it, but that thief was sort of cute.

SCENE SIX

NARRATOR: After that episode, the Pharaoh had new respect for the thief.

PHARAOH: Hmmm. That was a clever thing that young thief did. Maybe I should reconsider my attitude toward him. He's certainly smarter than any of the people I have working for me now.

PRINCESS: And I'm also reconsidering marrying that rich prince from Assyria you've set me up with. He's not as handsome or nearly as smart as that thief.

PHARAOH: Where's the Prime Minister?

DADAT: Here I am, at your service, sir!

PHARAOH: Issue a proclamation! If that thief comes forward, I'll give him amnesty. I'll make him part of my government. (*looking sadly at Dadat*) I desperately need some smart people in my government!

NARRATOR: Amazingly enough, Sety believed the Pharaoh.

MOTHER: It's just another trap, son. Don't fall for it.

SETY: I've got a feeling that the Pharaoh is serious. Besides, now that I've seen the Princess up close, I've got another incentive.

MOTHER: Suit yourself, but I think you should make another visit to the mortician.

NARRATOR: He walked right up to the palace and turned himself in to the guards. Within moments, he was standing before the Pharaoh.

SETY: It was I, Your Highness, who stole your gold and jewels together with my brother. I took his body from the palace gates and tricked your daughter. I ask for your forgiveness.

PHARAOH: Forgiveness? Forgiveness? Nonsense! I'll give you a reward instead. You can keep all the gold you stole, you can have a good job in the government, and you can marry my daughter!

PRINCESS: Hooray! Finally, I'll have someone I can talk to.

SETY: Thank you, Your Highness. You'll never regret this.

DADAT: This is wonderful, Pharaoh. You've suddenly become a forgiving and generous person. Part of your greatness is that you can change your mind, Your Highness.

PHARAOH: Change my mind? Don't be silly, Prime Minister. I'm not forgiving, and I'm certainly not generous. I just realized that this boy can make me lots of money! Who knows? He might make a great prime minister someday.

DADAT: I guess this would be the wrong time to bring up the issue of a raise.

THE END

TALK ABOUT IT

Tombstone

The Pharaoh in this story may seem selfish in his desire for a monument, but is he? Aren't tombs, statues, and plaques very important in our society today? Why do we build them, often at great public expense, and spend our vacations visiting them? What lessons do our monuments teach us?

The Rewards of Deception?

In this tale, a clever thief with a good heart is rewarded rather than punished. How realistic is this ending? Would a computer company hire a hacker to be chief of internet security? Ask students to consider other stories, such as the tales of Robin Hood, in which "thieves" are the heroes. What encourages us to root for the "bad guy" in these instances?

High-Level Adviser

If you were a prime minister, what advice would you give the ruler of your nation? Ask students to think of three pieces of advice they would give to any ruler, such as a pharaoh or president. You might want to discuss how writers like Niccolo Machiavelli (1469 – 1527) became famous by writing "self-help" books for would-be rulers.

EXTENSION ACTIVITIES

Become an Ancient Architect

Encourage students to try out their drawing and spatial relations skills. If they were in charge of building a pharaoh's tomb, what would it look like? How many chambers would it have? Would it have hidden chambers? Where would the ruler's stone coffin, known as the *sarcophagus*, be placed? Remind students that many of the tombs also contained traps, such as deep pits and blind tunnels, that were meant to thwart potential grave robbers. This assignment will afford you a good opportunity to show students pictures or diagrams of some of the famous tombs of Egypt.

Set the Agenda

Like most rulers, the Pharaoh in this story has many things on his mind. Ask students to imagine that they are rulers in ancient Egypt and invite them draw up a "to-do" list. Based on what you've read and discussed, ask them what events they would have to face in a given day. Which events would be top priorities? Helping the farmers? Waging war? Building a tomb? This list can also be incorporated into a letter-writing exercise in which the ruler describes his or her responsibilities to a prime minister.

 # THE STORY OF ISIS AND OSIRIS

CHARACTERS

- Scribe One
- Scribe Two
- Nut, the goddess of the earth
- Osiris, the god of the afterlife, the firstborn son of Nut
- Horus, god of light
- Set, the god of darkness and chaos

- Isis, the goddess of the moon and magic, the wife of Osiris
- Nephthys, the goddess of death
- Craftsman
- Girl
- Queen, the ruler of the city kingdom of Byblos (*BIB los*) in Phoenicia (*fo NEE she a*)

BACKGROUND

The story of Isis and Osiris is one of the best-known stories from Egyptian mythology. Like many of the ancient stories, it has different versions. This play is largely based on the version that was recorded by the Greek writer Plutarch (*PLU tark*), who lived in the first century A.D. It seems that there were followers of Isis and Osiris in ancient Greece as well!

As the story opens, it is about 2300 B.C. Two scribes sit in the shade in a temple courtyard in the Egyptian city of Thebes (*Theebs*). They are teachers and have finished with their work for the day, teaching their students how to write hieroglyphics (*hi RO glif iks*). As they chat, they begin to discuss their favorite subject: how great it is to be a scribe.

SCENE ONE

SCRIBE ONE: So then I said to that kid, "What? You want to join the army and drive a chariot! Are you crazy?"

SCRIBE TWO: Imagine that, wanting to be a charioteer rather than a scribe! After all we've told those knuckleheads, they still don't know how lucky they could have it.

SCRIBE ONE: I don't know what's so attractive about the army. Long, dusty rides in the desert, sitting behind a horse for long periods of time, having to duck all those arrows.

SCRIBE TWO: Just think, those kids could be scribes and get great jobs working for the government or even for the Pharaoh himself.

SCRIBE ONE: High pay, glamour, getting the inside scoop on all the government scandals. I told that boy he had a great career ahead of him, but he said our job is . . . is . . .

SCRIBE TWO: What? Too challenging? Too exciting?

SCRIBE ONE: Not exactly. He said our job was . . . boring.

SCRIBE TWO: Boring? Boring? That is an outrage! What did you say to that ungrateful brat?

SCRIBE ONE: I used the secret weapon . . . and then he swore he'd never be anything but a scribe.

SCRIBE TWO: What secret weapon was that?

SCRIBE ONE: The stories. I told him that scribes get to hear and write down stories. I told him the story of Isis and Osiris.

SCRIBE TWO: Oh, yes, Isis and Osiris. By the way, what story did you really use?

SCRIBE ONE: Stop kidding me. You *must* know the story. It's full of mystery, adventure . . . and it even has a happy ending.

SCRIBE TWO: Oh, sure, sure . . . I know it. Absolutely. But there are lots of different versions of the stories. Can you . . . can you tell me *your* version of the story?

SCRIBE ONE: Are you sure you are familiar with this material?

SCRIBE TWO: Well . . . sort of.

SCRIBE ONE: You don't know the story of Isis and Osiris? How did you get your scribe's license? Listen up while I tell you what you should already know.

SCENE TWO

SCRIBE ONE: Right around the beginning of time, give or take a few years, there was the goddess of the sky, and she was called Nut.

NUT: I gave birth to five gods on consecutive days. I know it sounds unlikely, but this is a myth, after all. Unlikely things happen all the time in myths.

OSIRIS: I was born first. And you know how everyone loves the firstborn. I'm told the common folk shouted "The lord of the Earth has been born" when I arrived on the scene. But I don't like to brag.

HORUS: I was the second in line. I am so glorious that people sometimes refer to me as "the face of heaven."

SET: *(impatiently)* Would you two just get over yourselves? You are always bragging!

NUT: Allow me to introduce my "problem child."

SET: Finally, the moment you were waiting for. Drum roll, please! Set is born. That's me. The god of chaos! How did they get along without me?

NUT: It wasn't too hard to get along without chaos.

SET: She's just saying that. My mother loves me so much that she didn't want me to be born and have an independent life. I had to jump out of her side instead of being born in the usual fashion. If I had waited around, I might never have been born.

ISIS: *(exasperated)* Quiet down, Set. You always need attention. *(collecting herself)* I, Isis, was the fourth-born. I have lots of powers—like magic and the wild wind.

NEPHTHYS: Don't forget about me, big sister. The last one born. I may be the youngest of Nut's five children, but that doesn't mean I'm a zero. I am the goddess of death, after all. *(pausing)* I know it's not a pleasant job, but someone has to do it.

SCRIBE ONE: Osiris soon proved that he was important and not just because he was the firstborn of the gods.

SCRIBE TWO: How? What exactly did Osiris do?

OSIRIS: I civilized the people of Egypt. First, I taught them to obey laws and have respect for one another. Also—so that they could survive—I taught them how to raise crops.

SCRIBE ONE: Not too shabby, especially since most of Egypt is desert.

SCRIBE TWO: True, learning how to farm on a small strip of land isn't an easy feat.

SCRIBE ONE: And Osiris did all this, not with force or bullying, but with common sense. He talked to the people . . . and they listened. The goddess Isis listened to him, too.

OSIRIS: My dear, let us be married. We'll make great partners and help turn Egypt into a great civilization.

ISIS: I do . . . and we will.

SCRIBE ONE: There was great rejoicing when Isis and Osiris married. The heavens were filled with shouts of joy. Well . . . almost filled.

SET: It makes me sick. Everyone loves Osiris, and now everyone loves the first couple. Osiris gets the big temples and all the attention. The rest of us gods get dusty little temples in tiny villages. This situation calls for a little chaos.

SCENE THREE

SCRIBE ONE: Set cooked up a plot that would bring Osiris down from his high place. He didn't care that Osiris had helped the Egyptians survive and thrive in the desert.

SET: I'll use Osiris's own vanity to trick him. Here's what I'll do. I'll make a beautiful box—the most beautiful box in the world—and I'll let Osiris do the rest. I'll have to make sure Isis is out of the way, though. She's too smart for my plot.

SCRIBE ONE: Set used all his powers to build a chest out of beautiful wood. He ordered artists to carve hunting scenes into the wood and then set precious stones in it.

SET: Here are my orders. Follow them exactly . . . or else!

CRAFTSMAN: Boss, I've got one question. How big should this chest be?

SET: Get the measurements from Osiris's tailor.

CRAFTSMAN: Oh, is this going to be a closet for the greatest of the gods!

SET: Not exactly, and drop all that "greatest of the gods" stuff.

SCRIBE ONE: One night, while Osiris was hosting a dinner party—one that Isis did not attend—Set appeared with the beautiful chest.

SET: My dear fellow god, I'm so sorry to interrupt your little party, but I just had to show you something. Do you see what I was able to get my artists to do?

SCRIBE ONE: The crowd "ooohed" and "aaahed" when they saw the beautiful box. All those in the room wanted it for themselves.

SET: Now, Osiris, just to show how generous I am, especially with you and your friends, I am going to give this chest away—that's right, I am going to give this away, but for a limited time only—to whoever can fit inside.

SCRIBE ONE: All the dinner guests dropped their food and rushed toward the box. Osiris himself wanted to go, but he didn't.

OSIRIS: *(speaking to himself)* That's the most beautiful box I've ever seen. I should have it, but it would seem undignified for me to join the mob. I'll play it cool.

SCRIBE TWO: I bet Set had planned for that, too.

SCRIBE ONE: You're right!

SET: Isn't this interesting? No one fits the box just right. Some of you are too small, and some are too big. I think that many of you should think twice before having seconds at these banquets. Everyone's given the box a try, except for you, Osiris.

SCRIBE ONE: With that, all the diners started to chant. "Osiris, Osiris, Osiris," they called until the god smiled and stood up to try out the box.

SET: *(helping Osiris get inside the box)* I have a feeling this is going to be a perfect fit. Are you comfy?

OSIRIS: *(stretching out)* Oh, yes. You know, this feels as though it was tailor-made for me.

SET: What an interesting thought!

SCRIBE ONE: As quickly as he could, Set gave a signal and his henchmen rushed up to the chest. In a flash they nailed the cover on, trapping Osiris inside. Then, to make sure he wouldn't get out, they poured hot lead over the box to seal it closed.

SCRIBE TWO: Why, Osiris probably couldn't breathe in there.

SCRIBE ONE: I'm afraid that was Set's plan . . . but not the only part of his plan.

SET: Take it to the Nile and throw it in. Let the river rid us of this know-it-all god. From now on, I'm in charge here.

SCRIBE TWO: Things seem pretty bleak!

SCRIBE ONE: Don't give up hope yet! The story's just beginning.

SCENE FOUR

SCRIBE TWO: Let me see if I can recall what happened next. Don't tell me. Isis began to wonder what happened to Osiris . . . .

ISIS: I haven't seen my beloved for days, ever since he was at that dinner party. I'm beginning to get worried. I wonder if that Set has . . .

SET: Mention my name and I'll appear!

ISIS: My husband is missing, and I think you have something to do with it!

SET: Me! Everyone blames me for everything, just because I'm the god of chaos. Is that fair? Your husband runs off, and suddenly it's my fault!

ISIS: I'm sorry, but it just seemed natural to blame you. You and he didn't exactly see eye to eye.

SET: I accept your apology. As your new leader, I think it's important to forgive and forget.

ISIS: New leader?

SET: Yes. I'm filling in for Osiris, who seems to have run away from his job. Too much pressure for the old boy, I guess.

ISIS: You're terrible! Just wait until Osiris comes back.

SET: I've got a feeling I'll be waiting a very long time for that!

SCRIBE ONE: Isis grew tired of waiting for Osiris to return home, so she set out to find him. She traveled in disguise far and wide across Egypt, hoping to find her husband. Finally, she came to a village at the very end of the Nile, just where the great river meets the sea.

SCRIBE TWO: Where she met—I remember now—a little girl!

ISIS: (*in an old woman's voice*) My dear, tell me, have any of the gods visited this place recently? Have you, perhaps, seen the great god Osiris?

GIRL: No, grandmother. Almost nothing happens in our village. Why, the magnificent box was the biggest news in years.

ISIS: The magnificent box? (*becoming interested*) Tell me about it!

GIRL: Well, it was big—big enough for someone to fit inside. It was beautiful but all sealed up. We were going to open it and look for jewels, but someone recognized the mark of Set on it, and we put it back in the water right away. There was also something else . . . .

ISIS: Tell me everything.

GIRL: Everyone who got near the box said it gave off powerful energy!

ISIS: *(agitated)* Quickly, tell me where the box went. The contents of that box are very special to me.

SCRIBE ONE: Isis followed the currents of the sea to the city of Byblos in Phoenicia. She learned that the box had come ashore beside a small bush. The energy from Osiris's body caused the bush to grow into a great tree. Soon the tree grew around the box completely, and it kept growing. It became one of the greatest trees in the kingdom.

SCRIBE TWO: When Isis arrived on the scene, she discovered that the King and Queen of the city had taken the tree to be a pillar in their palace. But Isis still didn't give up.

ISIS: I'll get a job in the palace and plan my next move. After all, I just can't walk in and tear the beam down.

SCRIBE ONE: It just so happened that the Queen needed someone to take care of her infant son, the Prince. Isis, disguised again as an old woman, was hired right away.

ISIS: The King and Queen are good people. I'll do something special for them before I ask for the tree trunk back. I'll use my magic fire to make their son immortal.

SCRIBE TWO: She placed the baby in the magical fire, which did not burn him but would have prevented any enemy or disease from harming him. But, just as the spell was beginning to work, the Queen walked in.

QUEEN: A fire! My baby! Help! What's going on here? You horrible witch, what have you done to my child?

ISIS: *(frustrated)* Your child is fine, but he'll never be immortal. You've broken my spell, and, by the way, I am the goddess Isis!

QUEEN: Oh, goddess, forgive me. Don't be offended! I was just afraid for my son's life. Don't punish us! Let us make it up to you in some way. Whatever you want is yours!

ISIS: Well, there is a rather large piece of wood that I'm interested in . . . .

SCRIBE ONE: Isis got the tree trunk from the palace. She cut through the wood and discovered Osiris's body. She brought her husband's body back to Egypt and hid it along the Nile.

ISIS: Now, I'll show everyone Set's dastardly work.

SCRIBE TWO: However, Set, who wanted to stay in power as long as possible, had other plans.

SET: Isis has been gone a long time. That snoop could find something that might make life difficult for me. I'd better look around and see what I can see.

SCRIBE ONE: As luck would have it, Set stumbled upon the right place.

SET: What's this hidden in the reeds? A box, a very familiar box. *(looking inside)* Isis has found the body, but she'll never use it as evidence against me. They'll never find Osiris now!

SCRIBE TWO: The evil Set tore the body of Osiris into bits and scattered them all around Egypt.

SET: I think we've seen the end of Osiris!

SCRIBE ONE: When Isis returned and could not find Osiris, she was beside herself.

ISIS: Has my husband's body disappeared again? What will happen to him in the afterlife? I must ask the other gods for help! Can anyone tell me what has happened?

NEPHTHYS: Sister, I can! Set has scattered the body across the land.

ISIS: Then I must find it. I will not rest until Osiris can rest.

SCRIBE ONE: Isis traveled throughout the land, searching for Osiris. Wherever she found a bit of him, she dedicated a temple to his memory. Some say, when she had gathered all the bits of his body together, she buried him.

SCRIBE TWO: That explains why there are so many temples to Osiris throughout the land!

SCRIBE ONE: Exactly! Remember, though, that's not the end of the story! Osiris surpassed Set after all.

SCRIBE TWO: He did? He had been killed and torn apart! How could he win?

SCRIBE ONE: Osiris became the lord of the afterlife, ruling over all the countless dead. He became much more powerful than Set.

SCRIBE TWO: Oh, I love a happy ending!

THE END

TALK ABOUT IT

Who Asked Them to the Party?

Osiris is the god of agriculture and later also becomes the god of the afterlife. These are important aspects of life. Why is Set, the god of chaos, also included in the family of gods? Why is Nephthys, the goddess of death, there as well? Are chaos and death to be respected, too? Why?

Leading Lady

Isis plays a major role in this story. What characteristics make her strong? If Isis were a character in a modern story, what would she be like? If there were a movie version of the story of Isis and Osiris, which famous actress should play the leading role?

Incognito

When gods in the ancient world appear to mortals, they tend to use disguises. Why? Are the gods afraid of the reaction they'll get from humans? Are they worried for the safety of common people? Make a list of possible reasons for gods to hide their identities.

EXTENSION ACTIVITIES

Help Wanted

Ask students to write a job description for a god or goddess, similar to one you might see in the "help wanted" section of your local newspaper. (*You might want to expand this assignment to include Greek and Roman deities along with the Egyptian gods.*) What characteristics should that god or goddess have? What tasks will the god or goddess be expected to perform? Then, ask students to take on the roles of gods and answer the ads. By combining the class's material, you will create a useful handbook of gods.

Picture This

Ask students to draw rough sketches of the gods in this story. Encourage students to give the gods special visual characteristics that will hint at their identity. Then, compare your students' pictures with representations of the gods taken from ancient Egyptian sources.
(*A number of books with pictures of Egyptian gods may be in your school or public library. You can start with the books listed in the bibliography at the end of this book.*)

Family Tree

At times, it seems that the gods are very much like a human family. As a creative writing assignment, ask students, to take the members of their own family and turn them into gods. Have students pick four or five family members or close friends and, in a series of short paragraphs, endow them with superhuman powers. (*Students can have fun turning the real-life qualities of family members into the extraordinary powers of gods.*)

THE SHIPWRECKED SAILOR

CHARACTERS

- Narrator
- Ambassador, one of the Pharaoh's most important messengers
- Imeny (*e MEN e*), an elderly sailor
- Pharaoh, the king of Egypt

- Sailor One
- Sailor Two
- Snake, a huge and magical reptile
- Sailor Three
- Sailor Four

BACKGROUND

About 4,000 years ago, during a time that is now known as the Middle Kingdom, the power and influence of Egypt expanded a great deal. At this time the pharaoh began to rule lands to the south, farther into the continent of Africa. Royal envoys and trade representatives were sent to distant lands to bring back gold, ivory, and other valuable goods to the court of the pharaoh. They brought back not only wonderful objects but also great stories. This folk tale, with its exotic treasures and its fantastic foreign lands, survives from that long-ago time.

SCENE ONE

NARRATOR: The Pharaoh's envoy stood in the rocking boat, looking out into the water of the Nile River and shaking his head.

AMBASSADOR: Should I jump in and drown myself now or wait until after lunch?

NARRATOR: He was not having a good day.

AMBASSADOR: With our cook, lunch is never too exciting. I might as well jump now.

NARRATOR: The Ambassador climbed up on the bow of the boat. He was trying to decide what sort of dive he should make—it would be his last one!—and hoping that he would not make a belly flop. Suddenly, an old sailor named Imeny came up beside him.

IMENY: Taking a dip before lunch, Your Excellency?

AMBASSADOR: Don't try to stop me. I've made up my mind. Goodbye, cruel world!

IMENY: Say hello to the crocodiles for me!

AMBASSADOR: *(with an expression of horror on his face)* What? Did you say crocodiles? You are just trying to distract me! Leave me alone. I am about to drown myself.

IMENY: Well, you'll get plenty of help. The minute you hit the water, the crocs will be racing to get you. First, they'll drag you down to the bottom. Then things will get ugly. They'll all want to get the first bite. I guess it's the juiciest. Oh, don't let me stop you. I suppose it's lunchtime for the crocodiles, too.

AMBASSADOR: But, I don't want to get bitten.

IMENY: Not just bitten. You'll be snapped at and chewed up into tiny pieces. The little baby crocs will nibble on your bones. Tomorrow they'll have leftovers. *(looking at the Ambassador's skinny legs)* On second thought, you might be just one serving.

AMBASSADOR: But . . . that sounds painful and gross. I just want to die peacefully. I don't want to be part of a crocodile food fight.

IMENY: Well, I don't blame you. Let's talk about that. Come back into the boat and sit down.

NARRATOR: The ambassador was a bit embarrassed but also relieved when he climbed back down to the deck. He sat down, and the old sailor sat next to him.

IMENY: First things first. Why don't you tell me why a successful and powerful man like yourself—one of the Pharaoh's chief messengers and traders, no less!—would want to jump into the Nile.

AMBASSADOR: Well, it's like this. A month ago, the Pharaoh himself called me to his palace, an amazing place of jewels and gold. I stretched out on the floor in front of the throne, and I heard his sacred command.

PHARAOH: Go south to Nubia and the Sudan. Bring back strange animals, beautiful plants, skins, pelts, ivory, and all the beautiful things you can fit in a ship.

IMENY: I see. His birthday is coming up, and he wants to give himself something special.

AMBASSADOR: Right! But the people down there were angry at us for some small war or something. People are so touchy! No trades, they said. In case you haven't noticed, our ship is empty.

IMENY: Meanwhile, the Pharaoh is expecting us to arrive in a boat that's practically sinking with treasure.

AMBASSADOR: Right. (*looking over the side of the boat again*) Maybe I should give myself to the crocodiles. After all, for failing at this job, the Pharaoh will have me tortured. Then he'll throw me to the crocodiles. I might as well do it myself!

IMENY: Wait a minute. You've got to look on the bright side of all this.

AMBASSADOR: Which is?

IMENY: Which is this: We are alive. We've returned from a long voyage to our beloved Egypt safe and sound.

AMBASSADOR: I suppose so.

IMENY: Besides, you don't know what kind of mood the Pharaoh will be in when we arrive. He may have completely forgotten about the treasure! Perhaps he'll be too busy to punish you. You aren't the only useless government official in our land, after all.

AMBASSADOR: (*beginning to lighten up*) You've got a point there. Maybe you are right!

IMENY: Of course I am. Be positive. Just being alive is a great gift.

AMBASSADOR: It is! Hey, for a lowly sailor, you are very wise. Has sailing up and down the Nile taught you all this?

IMENY: I don't take anything for granted now. Believe me, I've gone on voyages that nearly cost my life. Why, once I was the only member of the crew to survive.

AMBASSADOR: Really? What happened?

IMENY: If you promise to forget all about drowning, I'll tell you.

AMBASSADOR: It's a deal.

SCENE TWO

NARRATOR: The sailor launched into his story. As he listened, the Ambassador began to forget about his troubles.

IMENY: When I was much younger, without much experience in sailing, I got a job on one of the ships going to the Pharaoh's gold mines.

AMBASSADOR: You mean you had to travel on the dreaded Red Sea?

IMENY: Exactly. I was scared stiff because I had heard all kinds of stories about storms and sea monsters. I mean, once you get out of sight of land, there is no telling what will happen. But the other crew members, who were older and much more experienced, just laughed at me.

SAILOR ONE: *(to Imeny)* Stop shaking, you spineless child! Look at this boat! It's the best ship in the Pharaoh's entire navy. Nothing can sink it!

NARRATOR: The pharaohs always had some special boats for sea travel, ships that could withstand the currents and the fierce waves. These ships were larger and stronger than those used to navigate the Nile. Some were said to carry as many as one hundred crew members!

IMENY: But no matter what anyone told me, assuring me that nothing could sink the ship, I was scared stiff.

SAILOR TWO: We've made this trip plenty of times, you frightened little cat. The only danger is that you'll be so scared and shake so much that you'll sink the boat!

SAILOR ONE: Yeah, or maybe you'll sweat yourself to death!

SAILORS: *(together)* Ha! Ha! Ha!

IMENY: The only thing worse than being scared was being mocked. I just couldn't listen to that talk day in and day out. Though I was still scared, I made myself believe that I'd be safe with such a great boat and such a great crew. I didn't want to seem like a baby!

AMBASSADOR: What happened?

IMENY: Nothing, at first. Just as all of our sea-faring ships do, we tried to stay as close to the coastline as we could. Then, one day, we were caught in a terrible fog!

SAILOR ONE: How close are we to the land and the rocks?

SAILOR TWO: I don't know, but I think we should move a little further out so we don't end up crashing.

IMENY: By the time the fog lifted, we found ourselves out in the middle of the sea, completely lost. Each time we thought we were heading toward land, we ended up traveling farther out to sea!

AMBASSADOR: That's terrible! You must have been terrified.

IMENY: I was scared all right, but this is just the beginning of the story. It gets much worse!

SCENE THREE

IMENY: While we were in the middle of nowhere, a fierce storm appeared on the horizon. The winds began to whip our boat around as if it were a tiny twig.

AMBASSADOR: I bet the other crew members got scared then.

IMENY: Unfortunately for them, they didn't. I grabbed hold of a big piece of wood that was lying in the bow, but the other sailors just laughed at me. In fact, they were so busy talking that they didn't realize how bad it really was out there.

SAILOR ONE: (*speaking loudly to be heard above the wind*) This storm is nothing! Why, last year I was in storm so bad that I couldn't tell whether I was under or above the water.

SAILOR TWO: (*shouting to be heard*) Big deal! I was in a storm so bad that the ship was underwater and we had to hold our breath all day as we rowed.

SAILOR TWO: Oh, yeah? Well . . .

IMENY: They never got to finish their boasting and arguing.

AMBASSADOR: (*speaking hopefully*) You were rescued?

IMENY: No! A huge wave swallowed up our ship, and everything went dark. I thought I had died, but I realized that my fingernails were still stuck deep into that old piece of wood.

AMBASSADOR: You had survived!

IMENY: Just barely!

AMBASSADOR: And the rest of the crew?

IMENY: I am sorry to say that their spirits are probably still arguing in the afterlife.

AMBASSADOR: But then were you rescued from the high seas? Don't tell me you had to float around, with strange sea creatures nipping at your toes! Tell me you were saved right away.

IMENY: No, fate was not that kind to me, not yet at least. I floated all alone for three days. I was thirsty and starving. I saw sharks swim around me. They must have decided I wasn't worth the trouble. Finally, when my strength had just about run out, and I couldn't hold on for another moment, I was washed ashore on an island.

SCENE FOUR

AMBASSADOR: What island? Is there an island in the sea that Egypt doesn't control? I'll have to tell the Pharaoh this. What is the name of this island?

IMENY: You haven't heard of this island, I'm sure.

AMBASSADOR: Describe it to me.

IMENY: It was like a paradise. There were trees heavy with delicious fruit. Crystal-clear springs bubbled up everywhere, and waterfalls cascaded down from the hills. In one pond, fish jumped up into my waiting arms. They seemed eager for me to eat them.

AMBASSADOR: Perhaps we could turn it into some sort of vacation spot for the Pharaoh's ministers. We could call it "Pharaoh Land." Were the fish tasty?

IMENY: I'll never know. I built a fire so that I could cook the fish and make an offering to the gods. Whoever saved my life deserved thanks, I figured. The fire got good and hot, and I was just about to start cooking, when I heard a tremendous noise.

AMBASSADOR: *(becoming frightened)* It was the sound of waves crashing to the shore, I bet. Or maybe it was your imagination!

IMENY: No. The trees around me started to shake. The ground trembled. Suddenly, I was face to face with a gigantic snake!

AMBASSADOR: *(very upset)* Oh no, I hate snakes! Did he kill you? *(looking at Imeny)* No, I guess he didn't.

IMENY: This snake was about fifty feet long. He was covered with gold scales, and breathed fire.

SNAKE: *(in a deep but snake-like voice)* Tell me what you are doing on my island. You'd better speak quickly or I'll turn you into well-done barbecue.

NARRATOR: Imeny forgot to mention that the snake could speak human languages!

IMENY: Oh, yes! This snake spoke very well. Excellent grammar for a reptile!

AMBASSADOR: I noticed that he was very clear about blasting you with his fire.

IMENY: Of course, with that kind of pressure to speak, I couldn't think of a word to say. All I could do was stand there and shake. I had survived the shipwreck only to become some creature's lunch. I started to cry.

SNAKE: *(becoming nicer)* Calm down now! Don't go to pieces! Take a deep breath, forget that I might roast you at any moment, and explain why you are here.

IMENY: I opened my mouth, but nothing came out. I just figured my life was over.

SNAKE: Oh, stop it! I hate it when my meals become all stressed out. It makes the meat too tough. Listen, I'll give you a break, but don't let it get around that I'm a nice guy. But, for goodness' sake, calm down.

IMENY: The snake grabbed me gently in its jaws. I was caged inside its mouth. Soon I found myself in the snake's cave.

SNAKE: Welcome to my home. Don't let all the gold, ivory, and jewels fool you. I am really a very simple snake. However, you must tell me how you came to my island.

NARRATOR: Imeny did finally get his voice back, and he told the serpent about his sea voyage and how he alone survived the shipwreck.

IMENY: Then I made a fire to thank the gods for having saved me.

SNAKE: You were right. Some god must have been watching over you, for no one finds the way to my island without divine help.

IMENY: What sort of place is this?

SNAKE: This is Ka Island, but you can call it "Soul Island." I am its only resident.

IMENY: You live here all alone?

SNAKE: I am the last of my species. At one time, this island was full of snakes like me, my brothers and sisters.

IMENY: What happened to the rest of you?

SNAKE: One beautiful night, all of us left our caves to sleep in the moonlight. All, except me. I never cared for camping and I stayed in my cozy cave. A bright star fell from the sky and crashed into our island. Everyone perished but me.

IMENY: You must be very sad and lonely.

SNAKE: At times I feel the bite of sadness, but I have my life, and life is good. I feel lucky to be alive and I was able to help you.

IMENY: Life is good. Even when everything seemed dark and hopeless, you never despaired. I'll always remember that.

SNAKE: Perhaps you can pass that idea on to some of your fellow creatures when you return to your home.

IMENY: If I ever get home, you mean. I'll probably end my days right here, in paradise, eating fruit and chatting with a gigantic snake.

SNAKE: Oh, no, you won't. I can foresee the future. Did I forget to mention that?

IMENY: You were being such a good host, it probably slipped your mind.

SNAKE: I foresee that you'll be here for only four months. Then you'll be rescued. When your death does come, it will be gentle. You'll be in your own village in Egypt, surrounded by your family. I know how important a proper burial is for you Egyptians.

IMENY: What will I do with myself for four months?

SNAKE: Think of this as a vacation. You can enjoy the pleasures of my island until then. And when you return home, I will give you great gifts to take back to your king, the Pharaoh. But my greatest gift to you will be this message: Never give up hope.

IMENY: You've been so generous. I promise to return to this island and repay you for your kindness.

SNAKE: Thank you, but that won't be necessary, or possible. You'll understand later.

SCENE FIVE

NARRATOR: The snake's word was true. Exactly four months after Imeny washed up on shore, a ship that had been blown off course passed right by the island. Imeny ran down to the beach to greet the sailors. On the beach was a pile of treasure, including fragrant incense, precious oils, and ivory. The snake had left the treasure there as a parting gift.

IMENY: *(shouting to Sailors)* Welcome to Ka Island!

SAILOR THREE: Thank you, but where are we?

SAILOR FOUR: We were sailing back from the Pharaoh's gold mines, and we suddenly were surrounded by thick fog. When the fog lifted, we saw your island.

IMENY: It's not my island. It belongs to the snake.

SAILOR THREE: The snake? A snake owns this whole island?

IMENY: Not just any snake. He's huge, about fifty feet long, has golden scales, breathes fire, and speaks wonderfully, but he doesn't like camping and . . .

SAILOR FOUR: *(whispering to the other Sailor)* This guy has been out in the sun too much. Either that or we're about to meet one mean creature. Let's get off this island right now.

SAILOR THREE: *(whispering back)* After a while, all these castaways start imagining things. It happens all the time. *(to Imeny)* Excuse me, we'd love to stay and meet your . . . um . . . friend, but we've got to shove off. If you're coming with us, you've got to get on board.

IMENY: But I've got to say goodbye to the snake.

SAILOR FOUR: I'm sure the snake will understand. Can we give you a hand with your treasure?

IMENY: I guess so. *(shouting out as he leaves the island)* Thank you for everything! I'll never forget what you have taught me about life!

NARRATOR: They boarded the ship. A mysterious current took the ship away from the island and back toward Egypt.

SAILOR THREE: Hey, look back at the island!

SAILOR FOUR: I can't believe it! The whole island is sinking!

NARRATOR: In the distance, the sea bubbled, and the island began to disappear. In a moment, only the treetops were visible, then nothing.

IMENY: (*speaking softly*) Goodbye, my friend! I'll never forget what you told me.

SCENE SIX

IMENY: So, you see, I've been through some adventures, but I've never given up. Life itself is a gift.

AMBASSADOR: What happened when you got back?

IMENY: Well, I tried telling everyone I met what I learned from the snake, but nobody seemed to listen. Either they were too busy, or they thought I was crazy.

AMBASSADOR: What about the treasure?

IMENY: Easy come, easy go. Some of it was stolen by the crew. I gave the rest of it to the Pharaoh.

AMBASSADOR: You met the Pharaoh!

IMENY: This was a long time ago. The Pharaoh back then—it must have been the father or grandfather of the present Pharaoh—gave me a medal. I had the medal for a while, but I lost it.

AMBASSADOR: (*amazed*) You lost it!

IMENY: I guess treasures just aren't very important to me.

AMBASSADOR: You are an amazing person! You've certainly changed my mind. I'm going to live and meet the Pharaoh face to face. I'll just tell him the truth. There will be no treasures from my mission.

IMENY: That's the spirit, but . . . may I suggest something?

AMBASSADOR: Certainly!

IMENY: If the Pharaoh does get angry at you, try telling him about the shipwrecked sailor you met. This story has a way of changing a person's attitude.

THE END

AFTER READING

TALK ABOUT IT

Stories within Stories
"The Shipwrecked Sailor" is really a story about stories. How many smaller stories contribute to the larger tale? Does the story-within-a-story phenomenon also exist in the stories we tell every day? What is the difference between simple stories and complex stories?

Water Works
This story stresses the importance of the Nile River and the Red Sea in the life of Egypt. List the reasons that these two bodies of water were and still are very important for Egyptians.

Fear of the Unknown
The Shipwrecked Sailor story comes from a period of time when the Egyptians were venturing outside their own country to explore and trade with distant and unfamiliar lands. What does this story say about their hopes and fears? What countries do the students consider "distant" today?

A Tall Tale
Discuss the difference between fantasy and reality. Which elements of the story are clearly imaginative? Which are very realistic? Why did the storyteller include the unbelievable parts?

EXTENSION ACTIVITIES

The Power of Stories
Words have the power to transform people. Stories can calm us down or fill us with excitement. In *The Arabian Nights*, a young woman uses tales to fascinate the king and thereby save her life. Which stories—from fiction, history, or family history—have meant the most to your students. Why? You may even want to organize a storytelling day in which students get a chance to share their favorites.

The Price of Riches
In this story, the Ambassador worries about not having treasure, but Imeny seems to care little about wealth. Take a few moments to ask students about the message of this play. What do they value most? Why? Try asking students about the toys that they were desperate to buy as younger children. Where are those toys now? What other "toys" or wealth do they long for now? What things always remain valuable?

An Enchanted Island
Ask your students to imagine their own perfect "islands." You might want to introduce the idea of a utopia. Although the word is generally understood as meaning "perfect place," its literal meaning is "no place." Ask students what they would include in their utopias. Using their lists as rough outlines, students can write descriptive paragraphs. If time allows, ask students to draw maps of their magical islands.

 # HELEN OF EGYPT

CHARACTERS

- Narrator One
- Kherheb (*CUR heb*), devoted to serving the gods of ancient Egypt
- Herodotus (*he ROD a tus*), a Greek historian conducting research in Egypt in ancient times
- Menelaus (*men e LAY us*), king of Sparta, Helen's husband
- Helen, the mortal daughter of Zeus, the most beautiful woman in world
- Narrator Two

- Paris, a prince from the ancient city kingdom of Troy
- Aphrodite (*af ro DI tee*), the Greek goddess of love
- Crew Member
- Governor, the government official in charge of a small area in Egypt
- Pharaoh, the king of Egypt, who was believed to be a god

BACKGROUND

According to the *Iliad*, a famous epic poem written by the Greek poet Homer, there was once a great war between the people of Greece and the people who lived in the city of Troy. Today scholars believe that such a war may have taken place about 1250 B.C. The *Iliad* tells us that all the fighting started over a woman named Helen, who had been kidnapped from Sparta in Greece and brought to Troy by a prince named Paris. It is said that Helen was so beautiful that her face "launched a thousand ships." What that phrase means is that many of the kings who lived in Greece at that time put together a great fleet and sailed to Troy to bring Helen back home. The Trojans were not willing to return Helen to her husband, Menelaus, and her countrymen. A ten-year war followed. Ultimately, the Greeks won, and Helen was brought back to Greece by Menelaus to live with him.

    The ancient Egyptians had a very different version of the story, and that version is presented in this play. This story was told by the priests of Egypt until it was written down by the Greek historian Herodotus, who went to Egypt to learn more about the past. (When the Greeks wanted to study ancient history, they went to Egypt. Though Greek civilization is old, the kingdoms of Egypt stretch much further back into the sands of time.)

SCENE ONE

NARRATOR ONE: It is 450 B.C. A visitor from Greece, the historian Herodotus, has come to see the ancient pyramids of Egypt. He's doing research for his great history book. Just imagine what it was like to be a tourist 2,400 years ago. On his visit to the three great pyramids of Giza, near what is now the city of Cairo, Herodotus meets Kherheb, a priest, who becomes his guide.

KHERHEB: Well, have you seen enough of these three tombs?

HERODOTUS: No, I want to spend several weeks looking at them. I want to report back to my people just how impressive they are.

KHERHEB: If you spend too much time here, though, you may never get to see our other temples, pyramids, and statues.

HERODOTUS: You mean you have more?

KHERHEB: My dear man, these three tombs are just the tip of what we have in our land. You must take a boat up the Nile to the city of Thebes.

HERODOTUS: Wait, don't you mean "down the Nile"? On my map here, we'd be traveling south and we call that down.

KHERHEB: The Nile flows from south to north. Therefore, when you go south, you're going "up" the Nile.

HERODOTUS: I guess I've got a lot to learn.

KHERHEB: Getting back to Thebes, it's there that you'll find the Temple of Luxor. I'm sure you Greeks have nothing like it at home. Make sure your bring a postcard back with you. You might even be able to bring back a souvenir. My cousin has a shop . . .

HERODOTUS: (*becoming jealous*) Well, you Egyptians might be great at building things, but we Greeks are way ahead in other things.

KHERHEB: Such as . . . ?

HERODOTUS: Such as literature. We've got these great stories that you haven't even heard of.

KHERHEB: Go ahead. I'm listening.

HERODOTUS: Well, like the whole story of the Trojan War. You didn't have a great poet like Homer. He wrote some terrific poems—very long but still terrific—about that war. I had to learn some of his poetry by heart. Want to hear some? (*putting on a serious voice*) "O goddess, sing of the destructive anger of Achilles, the son of Peleus, which . . ."

KHERHEB: (*rolling his eyes*) Wonderful, but no more, please. You don't want to lose your voice this early in your trip.

HERODOTUS: Don't you want to learn more about Homer and Helen and the gods and the battles?

KHERHEB: We've heard of your great poet. He certainly could compose great battle scenes, even though they are a bit too bloody for my taste. However, it's a terrible shame that he got it all wrong.

HERODOTUS: All wrong? What? What do you mean, "wrong"? You can't say that about Homer! He's one of our national heroes!

KHERHEB: I'm so sorry that I've upset you. I'm not being a good host. I shouldn't have said that Homer got it "wrong." It's just that here in Egypt, we've got our own version of what happened to Helen, her husband, and all those who fought in the war.

HERODOTUS: If you are apologizing, I accept on behalf of my country. Now, be so kind as to tell me *your* version of the Trojan War.

KHERHEB: With pleasure.

SCENE TWO

NARRATOR ONE: It all started in a place called Sparta. There was a great king, Menelaus, and his wife, Helen.

MENELAUS: I rule one of the greatest kingdoms in Greece and I'm married to the most beautiful woman in the world.

HELEN: Don't forget that Zeus is my father. Isn't it nice to have the king of the gods as your father-in-law?

MENELAUS: (*not paying attention*) What's that, my dear? Zeus? Oh, yes. Wonderful.

HELEN: Is something bothering you, my dear? You seem a bit distracted. Are you upset with your brother, Agamemnon, again? Put it out of your mind! He's just got family issues! He still thinks your father liked you better.

MENELAUS: No, my dear, it's not that.

HELEN: Well, then, what is it?

MENELAUS: Have you noticed that shepherd who's always hanging around the palace? The young man from Troy?

HELEN: You mean the one who seems to faint whenever I come into the room? His name is Paris.

MENELAUS: How do you know his name?

HELEN: Well, that's what he signs on his love letters! Of course, he could be using a fake name.

MENELAUS: (*sarcastically*) This is just great! My wife is getting love letters from a shepherd.

HELEN: Don't worry. He's only a boy. He's just got a crush on me. I don't take him seriously. Do you think I'd run off with a shepherd when I live in luxury in a palace?

MENELAUS: Well, that's not the only reason I don't like him.

HELEN: What else is wrong?

MENELAUS: He's a lousy shepherd. He's too busy writing love letters and not spending enough time watching the sheep!

NARRATOR TWO: But Helen and her husband didn't know who Paris really was. He might have looked like a shepherd, but he was actually a prince of Troy.

NARRATOR ONE: Yes, and a very spoiled prince at that. He was used to getting what he wanted.

PARIS: I deserve the most beautiful wife in the world. Who cares if she's already married to someone else? Aphrodite, goddess of love, you promised to give me Helen. It's time you kept your end of the bargain. I'm going to hold my breath until you do!

APHRODITE: Calm down, my cute little mortal man. You chose me over those two other goddesses, Athena and Hera, and gave me the golden apple inscribed "To the most beautiful!," which we all claimed to be.

PARIS: (*making noises as he holds his breath*) Mmmm-mmm-mm.

APHRODITE: All right! All right! I'll cast a spell over her, but you've got to get her back to Troy. I can't do everything for you!

NARRATOR TWO: Troy was located in what people in the twenty-first century A.D. call the country of Turkey.

NARRATOR ONE: On a dark night, Paris hired some criminals to help him kidnap Helen. While Menelaus slept, Paris had Helen put on board a ship and then set sail on the darkened sea.

PARIS: I've stolen a ship, collected a crew of desperate criminals, and now I've kidnapped a bride for myself. I hope I get home to Troy soon, because I'm not going to be very popular around here.

APHRODITE: But Paris, remember that Troy isn't a hop, skip, and a jump from Sparta. Don't forget, the Aegean Sea can be tricky, too!

SCENE THREE

PARIS: I've never seen such winds and high seas! Forget about reaching Troy. We'll be lucky if we make it to shore alive.

CREW MEMBER: Hey, Paris, you promised us gold for helping you. You said that your father, Priam, the king of Troy, would honor us. You didn't tell us that we were going to drown.

KHERHEB: And the nearest shore happened to be . . . you guessed it . . . Egypt!

HERODOTUS: You mean Paris never took Helen to Troy? How can she be called Helen of Troy? What about Homer's big poem?

KHERHEB: Remember, this is the Egyptian version of the story! When Paris's ship washed up on shore, he didn't know where he was.

PARIS: Well, it's not Troy, and that's bad. But it's not Sparta, and that's good. (*speaking to Helen*) I bet your husband is hopping mad at me right now.

HELEN: Not just mad! When he finds out you're a Trojan prince, he's going to round up the best warriors in Greece and tear your city down.

PARIS: (*to himself*) Hmmm! I wonder if it's too late to take her back and tell Menelaus it was all just a big joke.

KHERHEB: The ship landed in Egypt, near the Nile River, within sight of a special temple.

HERODOTUS: Special?

KHERHEB: Yes, in Egypt we have many such temples. At this particular temple, any servant with an unjust master could seek sanctuary.

HERODOTUS: Wow, a slave could be protected from his evil master there!

KHERHEB: Yes. Naturally, Paris's crew decided this was a great place to jump ship.

CREW MEMBER: Let's leave this unlucky ship and save our lives!

PARIS: Oh, guys, come on back. I'll double your wages as soon as we get to Troy.

CREW MEMBER: (*sarcastically*) Oh, right! We'll drown before we see any of your money. Just try to sail your ship by yourself.

KHERHEB: The crew members sought sanctuary inside the temple and told anyone who would listen how Paris had stolen Helen away from her husband. Eventually, the sorry tale reached the ear of the local Governor.

GOVERNOR: (*seeming outraged*) What Paris did is a terrible scandal! A disgrace! (*beginning to smile*) I can't wait to tell the Pharaoh about this. He loves juicy gossip!

HERODOTUS: I'll bet the Pharaoh was too busy to worry about such a little story.

KHERHEB: Wrong! The Pharaoh forgot about all his other concerns—a new drought, an uprising among some people in the south, overseeing the construction of his tomb—and gave the affair his full attention.

PHARAOH: Send a letter to the Governor. Tell him to arrest Paris. Send everyone up the Nile to my capital here at Memphis so that I may hear about this case from the people themselves. (*to himself*) Just what I need . . . a scandal to take my mind off my boring work!

KHERHEB: Then the Governor set out to take the Greeks and Paris up the Nile, under an armed escort, of course, to the palace of the Pharaoh. Needless to say, Paris wasn't too happy about the trip.

PARIS: (*to Governor*) Look, Gov—you don't mind if I call you that, do you?—I don't want to take up any more of your precious time. I'll just take my . . . my friend Helen, and we'll find our own way. Thanks for the memories.

GOVERNOR: Forget about it! This is bigger than all of us now. We're off to see the Pharaoh. He's a living god, and there's no weaseling out of his commands! Just get in the boat and be quiet.

SCENE FOUR

KHERHEB: Paris and Helen headed south.

HERODOTUS: Up the Nile!

KHERHEB: Good! You are learning your geography! Even the crew members agreed to leave the temple and tell the Pharaoh the truth. As the boats approached the palace of the Pharaoh, the passengers could see great statues of the gods.

HELEN: Gold and jewels glitter everywhere. I don't know what to say!

KHERHEB: Soon everyone was silent, stunned by the wealth and power that they saw.

GOVERNOR: Paris, I hope you are truthful to our leader. Answer all of his questions completely and honestly.

PARIS: Of course. When was I anything but completely honest?

CREW MEMBERS: Let's see . . . Yesterday!

HELEN: And the day before that, and . . .

PARIS: All right! I've turned over a new leaf. I am the prince of truth now.

GOVERNOR: We've arrived at the Pharaoh's hall. Walk behind me and keep your eyes lowered. Remember that the Pharaoh is a god who simply dwells among us mortals for a short time.

KHERHEB: They were brought before the Pharaoh's throne. The Pharaoh immediately started to question Paris.

PHARAOH: Let me get this straight. You were a guest at the house of Menelaus. He gave you hospitality, as all the gods—Greek and Egyptian—say that we should. He gave you food and shelter and asked only that you look over some of his flocks.

PARIS: Yes, that's right. The food was okay, but I was more used to the food at home in the palace at Troy. Oh, forget I said that. I meant to say in my mother's kitchen.

PHARAOH: Did you say palace? Are you a member of the royal family of Troy?

PARIS: Well . . . sort of. I'm a prince.

PHARAOH: A prince of Troy! Did you hide your true identity from Menelaus?

PARIS: Well, I never actually got around to telling him who I really was. There just was never a good time. Then I left in a bit of a hurry.

PHARAOH: You left and you took your host's wife with you?

PARIS: It was love at first sight, Your Highness. We were blinded by our love for each other.

HELEN: Blinded? I was *blindfolded*, and tied up, too. I was minding my own business, and then Aphrodite appeared. I was in a fog. Suddenly, I was being carried to a ship! I was kidnapped!

PARIS: *Kidnapped* is such a harsh word. It's so easy to get the wrong impression. Can't we just say I wanted to surprise Helen with a trip to my father's city of Troy?

PHARAOH: Silence! I'm disgusted by you, Paris! I'd order your execution, but since you are a traveler here on our shores, I cannot. The laws of the gods demand that I must protect you and all visitors. Don't tempt me, though, or I may overlook that rule!

PARIS: Oh, Pharaoh, you must listen to the gods when they tell you to protect a visitor. That's one of my favorite rules, especially now.

PHARAOH: But that rule doesn't prevent me from throwing you out of Egypt! It's a long walk across the desert, you know. I understand it's a long swim to Troy.

PARIS: Your Greatness, I'll just take my ship, my crew, and Helen. Let's go.

PHARAOH: Not so fast. The crew can do whatever they want to do. Helen stays here. You must return to your homeland.

HELEN: I'm free!

PARIS: I'm sunk! How do I get home without a crew?

PHARAOH: That's your problem.

SCENE FIVE

KHERHEB: Somehow—no one knows exactly how—Paris made it home to Troy. Helen remained in Egypt.

HERODOTUS: But, according to our great poet, Homer, Helen was taken to Troy. The Greeks came over to Troy to get her back. Menelaus and his brother, Agamemnon, were the leaders of the mission!

KHERHEB: That's not the way our version of the story goes. I hate to be the one to tell you this, but Helen was in Egypt all during the war.

HERODOTUS: Impossible! You mean that the whole Trojan War was a mistake? All the brave warriors, such as Achilles and Hector, fought and died over a woman who wasn't even there?

KHERHEB: I'm afraid that's right! All wars are silly, but the Trojan War might be the most ridiculous!

HERODOTUS: The great city of Troy was burned to the ground for nothing?

KHERHEB: Sadly, yes. When the Greeks arrived to take Helen back, Paris tried to tell them that she was in Egypt.

HERODOTUS: Oh, no! I bet they didn't believe him!

KHERHEB: That's right! Poor Paris—his lying finally caught up with him. It was only after they tore the city apart that the Greeks started to see the truth.

HERODOTUS: I'm sorry, but they are never going to believe me at home. I'm not sure that our people will appreciate the idea that Homer was wrong. Well, you might as well tell me how the story ends.

KHERHEB: Well, after the Greeks won the war and destroyed Troy, they realized that Helen was not in the city. They remembered that Paris had said Helen was in Egypt. They sent Menelaus down to Egypt to see if the story was true.

HERODOTUS: I'll bet he was surprised when he got to Memphis.

KHERHEB: Helen was waiting for him, and she seemed more beautiful than ever. The Pharaoh gave a big party for Helen and Menelaus.

HERODOTUS: Then they all lived happily ever after, right?

KHERHEB: Not quite. As Menelaus was leaving, he committed a grave crime, but that's another story . . . .

THE END

AFTER READING

TALK ABOUT IT

National Treasure

Herodotus is upset that there may be a different version of one of his country's greatest myths. What myths are very important to us? What stories are very important to our country? How would we feel if someone told a different version of one of those cherished myths?

The Price of a Lie

After a while, no one believes Paris. Discuss the idea of "credibility." What would happen to us if people stopped believing what we said? How would our daily lives change?

The Face of Love

Aphrodite is so eager to win the approval of the mortal Paris that she offers him Helen and so the whole story of the kidnapping begins. How do you suppose ancient people saw their gods? Did they appear and disappear? Did they look like beautiful humans? Did the gods stand for things that cannot be seen, such as love and wisdom?

EXTENSION ACTIVITIES

Yet Another Version

If the Greeks and the Egyptians had their own versions of the story of Helen of Troy, there's room for a third or fourth version as well. Ask students to work in small groups and come up with an outline for another story about Helen, Paris, and the Trojan War. Students may want to write their versions out or discuss their versions with the rest of the class. Offer students the option of writing plays based on their stories.

Mapmaker

Ask students to draw two maps of the Mediterranean Sea, including Greece, Egypt, and Turkey, the country where the ancient city of Troy was located. For the first map, which will be just a sketch, ask students to work without any reference works. Ask them to base this map only on how they think the countries are positioned. Have students discuss their maps. What assumptions did they make about the sizes and relative distances of the countries? Compare these creative renderings with an accurate map and make a list of the differences between them. Finally, suggest that students try their hand at creating a realistic map based on what you've discussed in class and reference atlases.

A Different Sort of Pharaoh: The Life of Hatshepsut

CHARACTERS

- Nut, the goddess of the sky
- Hathor (*HATH or*), the goddess of love
- Thutmose I (*TUT mose*), the Pharaoh, the king of Egypt
- Ahmose (*a MOZ*), the queen and wife of Thutmose I
- Senmut (*SEN mut*), a friend of Hatshepsut
- Hatshepsut (*hat SHEP sut*), the daughter of the Pharaoh

- Thutmose II, a later Pharaoh
- Egyptian One
- Egyptian Two
- Thutmose III, a later Pharaoh
- High Priest
- Soldier

BACKGROUND

Around 3,500 years ago, hundreds of years before the Greeks and the Trojans did battle outside the great city of Troy, the Egyptians were already looking back to the glory days of their civilization. At that time, an unusual leader emerged in Egypt who sought to help the land regain its former glory. This leader, Hatshepsut, didn't have an unusual background or style. She was special because she was a "she." Many people know about Cleopatra, the beguiling Egyptian leader who captivated Julius Caesar and Mark Antony. However, centuries before Cleopatra, there was Hatshepsut.

This story is based on the paintings and carvings from Queen Hatshepsut's own temple in Egypt and the ideas of those who have studied her rule.

SCENE ONE

NUT: I can't get over it.

HATHOR: Don't get over it. Just get mad.

NUT: Those male gods think they're so great, but the last time I checked, they were as immortal as we are.

HATHOR: You go, girl!

NUT: And it's not only gods who are all messed up with inequality. Those mortals have a thing or two to learn. They need to know that women can be powerful, too.

HATHOR: That's right! Look at Hatshepsut and her accomplishments. She was a powerful, smart ruler, but people overlook her. She's a role model for all of us—gods, mortals, even for that Cleopatra, who had the Romans twisted around her little finger.

NUT: Hatshepsut did use some tricks to get where she got.

HATHOR: She had to. The cards were stacked against her.

NUT: I suppose so. I just wish that more people knew about Hatshepsut and her story.

HATHOR: Well, here's our chance to spread the word about one of the women who became powerful in Egypt.

NUT: Okay, here goes. Pharaoh Thutmose I ruled Egypt around 1500 B.C. He thought he had it all: wealth, power, and a great army to back up whatever he said.

HATHOR: He was a tough man and he fought many battles to extend the empire of Egypt. Under his command, Egypt stretched from the far south, in what was called Nubia, to the Euphrates River in the east, and to the vast deserts of the west.

NUT: Countries sent Thutmose "tribute," or protection money, just to leave them alone.

HATHOR: Still, there was one thing bothering the great Pharaoh.

THUTMOSE I: Everything's great, but I'm miserable.

AHMOSE: What's wrong dear? You're not letting those rebels spoil your breakfast again, are you?

THUTMOSE I: No, no, it's not that. I'm upset that I've got no son.

AHMOSE: You have been looking a little pale lately. Perhaps a tan would help.

THUTMOSE I: No! Not sun! A son! A male child. Someone who'll take my place when I die. Otherwise, all my hard work and success will pass to some stranger.

AHMOSE: You've got a beautiful child, our daughter Hatshepsut. She's full of royal blood. Everyone says she's brilliant, and she'll make a great leader, just like her father.

THUTMOSE I: (*thinking out loud*) Well, she probably did pick up those good qualities from me, come to think of it. She does have my good looks and perhaps at least some of my intelligence. (*becoming agitated again*) Still . . . Still . . . she's not a boy.

AHMOSE: Yes, dear, we went over all that when she was born. Remember that I explained how boys and girls are different . . . ?

THUTMOSE I: (*getting even more frustrated*) I mean that I have to have a son follow me on the throne.

AHMOSE: Hatshepsut is so bright, though.

THUTMOSE I: It doesn't matter. I might like her. You might like her. However, the other powerful people and the high priests won't like her. Egypt just isn't ready for a female ruler. A woman tried to rule more than two hundred years ago, but her reign was shorter than a breath.

AHMOSE: Well, you do have a problem dear, because she's your only child.

THUTMOSE I: I'll just have to look elsewhere. I've got to have a distant relative somewhere. They always seem to appear when they want something.

AHMOSE: You can't put someone else's child on the throne when it's Hatshepsut's right.

THUTMOSE I: My dear, you've got to be realistic. This is how politics works.

AHMOSE: Maybe it's how it *doesn't* work.

THUTMOSE I: (*angrily*) I am the king of Egypt and the incarnation of the god Horus! If I wanted to, I could command the sun to stop shining. (*calming down and realizing that he's lost control*) Of course, I don't feel like stopping the sun just right now.

AHMOSE: (*sarcastically*) Of course, you couldn't be bothered.

THUTMOSE I: Listen, we'll marry Hatshepsut off to the new prince I'll pick as my successor. That way she'll be a queen, at least, and all my good qualities won't go to waste.

AHMOSE: (*to herself*) I just wish fairness were one of those great qualities.

SCENE TWO

NUT: While the Pharaoh and his Queen were battling over her future, Hatshepsut and her friend Senmut were in another corner of the palace trying to stump each other with math problems.

SENMUT: All right, like everyone else I'm amazed at how smart you are. You'll never get this, though.

HATSHEPSUT: Want to bet?

SENMUT: Suppose two thousand of our soldiers sail across the sea to fight our enemies. Along the way a great wind sinks the ships, but all the soldiers are safe. Now, assuming that each ship can carry one hundred soldiers and it takes a month to build a boat, and we can't build more than four ships at once, how long will it take you to complete the mission?

HATSHEPSUT: Ten seconds.

SENENMUT: Ten seconds! My teachers say that I'm dumb, but you must be even dumber. The way I figure it . . .

HATSHEPSUT: It shouldn't take a fool more than ten seconds to figure out that we should leave others alone. We should build up Egypt and engage in peaceful trade with foreign nations, not try to control every people we encounter.

SENMUT: You're right . . . again. When you're king of Egypt, you'll be able to make those things happen.

HATSHEPSUT: Oh, yeah, right. I've got as much chance of becoming pharaoh as you have of being appointed chief engineer. Still, I know I could do a good job. Hey, do you suppose they would make an exception and give a woman the top job?

SENMUT: I wouldn't hold my breath.

HATHOR: As they were speaking, Pharaoh Thutmose and Queen Ahmose entered the room.

THUTMOSE I: No need to throw yourself on the ground and grovel before me, though I am a living god. We're all family here. (*suddenly noticing Senmut*) Almost all family, I should say. (*speaking with disdain*) Oh, hello, Senmut.

AHMOSE: Your father has some important news for you, dear.

THUTMOSE I: Yes, very important news. (*looking at Senmut*) Very private news.

HATSHEPSUT: Father, Senmut is my best friend. I can't just dismiss him. It's rude.

SENMUT: *(hiding his shame)* No, your father is right. Besides, I had better be studying. My teachers expect me to fail my next math test, but I want to put up a little bit of a fight at least.

HATHOR: Senmut withdrew from the chamber and left Hatshepsut with her parents.

THUTMOSE I: I am overjoyed to announce that you will wear the crown of Egypt. The queen's crown, that is.

HATSHEPSUT: Well, thank you. I will do my best to be queen, when that time arises.

THUTMOSE I: Oh, there is one detail I left out. You're getting married.

HATSHEPSUT: Married? To whom?

THUTMOSE I: Oh, he seems like a nice sort of fellow. He's got many good qualities, I'm sure, but most important, he's male. When the time comes, he'll be the next pharaoh. He'll be called Thutmose II. *(to himself)* I do like the ring of that name.

HATSHEPSUT: My blood is one hundred percent royal. Am I supposed to forget that?

THUTMOSE I: Heavens no, don't forget it. Your royal blood will help your husband's claim to the throne. Let's say he's "regally challenged." With your help, he'll be a great ruler.

AHMOSE: He doesn't have the royal pedigree. That's where you come in.

HATSHEPSUT: Father . . .

THUTMOSE I: Enough. I've made up my mind. Just start planning the royal wedding. By the way, don't bother inviting your friend Senmut to the affair. I don't want the wrong sort of people there!

SCENE THREE

NUT: And, so they were married. Hatshepsut did her duty as a loyal princess, even though she believed in her heart that she could rule as well as any man.

HATHOR: Eventually, Thutmose I died. Although he hadn't treated Hatshepsut fairly, Thutmose had been a good king for Egypt, and the people were sad to hear that he had made the journey to the afterlife.

NUT: Hatshepsut's friend Senmut was never invited to the wedding because her father thought he was "the wrong sort of friend," but their friendship persisted. There were still moments when Hatshepsut and Senmut could meet and talk.

SENMUT: How's life around the palace?

HATSHEPSUT: It's getting pretty dull. My husband spends all his time trying to figure out solutions to big problems, while I am supposed to sit around and just look pretty.

SENMUT: *(smiling)* That's a big challenge for you.

HATSHEPSUT: Be quiet! Do you know what the worst thing is?

SENMUT: What?

HATSHEPSUT: My husband is working himself to death trying to figure out problems that I could solve in the blink of an eye—except that I can't tell him the answers. I'm not supposed to show that I'm smart.

SENMUT: What do you do, then?

HATSHEPSUT: I hint at the solutions. When he gets my hints, and sometimes that can take a long time, I tell him that he's a genius.

SENMUT: Doesn't that get frustrating? Don't you just want to speak up yourself?

HATSHEPSUT: Do crocodiles live in the Nile? The Pharaoh wouldn't be happy if the Queen suddenly started making decisions.

SENMUT: You know, it's sort of the same with me. I'm getting really good at math and building, but every time a job comes along to build a tomb or a statue, it always goes to someone else. I feel that I'm cursed!

HATSHEPSUT: My father must have put in a bad word for you before he went to the next world.

SENMUT: *(sounding agitated)* Oh, no. I think I hear your husband coming right now. I'm going to make myself scarce.

THUTMOSE II: Hatshepsut! I've been looking all over for you!

HATSHEPSUT: I'm right here, my lord and husband.

THUTMOSE II: I can't remember that brilliant idea I had about how to keep those poor people in Upper Egypt from rebelling. It came to me as we were talking this morning. After you left, I just couldn't recall my great solution.

HATSHEPSUT: You were going to order the building of some new temples on the Nile. That way, the people could have jobs and have more money to pay taxes, and you'd get the honor from the gods. Everyone would be happy. Remember?

THUTMOSE II: Of course. You know, sometimes I surprise myself. I sit up all night worrying, and then all of a sudden an idea pops into my head from nowhere.

HATSHEPSUT: *(pretending to be impressed)* Isn't that amazing!

NUT: In this fashion, the marriage continued, and Thutmose II came to be known throughout Egypt as a shrewd leader.

HATHOR: However, even the all-powerful Pharaoh can't avoid the arrows of illness. After only a few years on the throne, Thutmose II died and joined Thutmose I in the afterlife.

NUT: Hatshepsut was saddened by her husband's death, for she had become fond of him during their marriage, but she thought that this might be her big moment.

HATSHEPSUT: *(to Senmut)*, I am the daughter of a pharaoh and his queen. I am a queen myself. I am strong enough and smart enough to rule this empire and make it even greater than it is.

SENMUT: You know that, and I know that, but what about the priests and the other nobles? Are they ready for a female pharaoh?

HATSHEPSUT: They have no choice! I will rule, and you will be my adviser and chief builder.

SENMUT: I like the sound of that. Chief builder! Adviser to the Pharaoh. Your father will be turning in his tomb.

NUT: Sadly, Hatshepsut learned that there was another choice. Her husband had a son by another wife, and he was named the next pharaoh, even though he was only about ten years old!

HATSHEPSUT: *(angrily)* I'm not going to stand in the shadows anymore.

SENMUT: Right. Shall we arrange a little "accident" for the boy king? Perhaps he could fall off a boat during the crocodile feeding time. Wouldn't it be a shame if he visited the pyramids and a block of stone fell on him . . . strictly by accident, of course.

HATSHEPSUT: Sorry, murder isn't my style.

SENMUT: But it would be so easy!

HATSHEPSUT: It's not the boy's fault that he's being pushed in front of me. I'll convince the priests that he's not quite ready to rule yet. I'll keep the throne ready for him, for a little while.

SENMUT: Maybe it'll be for a long while.

HATSHEPSUT: Right. We'll use our brains to figure this thing out.

SCENE FOUR

HATHOR: She might not have been the strongest member of the royal family or the tallest, and she definitely wasn't of the required sex, but Hatshepsut had plenty of brains, and she knew how to use them.

HATSHEPSUT: It's done. We are in power.

SENMUT: Already? How?

HATSHEPSUT: Well, I convinced the royal family and the high priests that I would rule until the boy king got a bit older. I'm just keeping the throne warm for him.

SENMUT: *(sarcastically)* Wonderful. You'll get a taste of power, and then it will be snatched away from you. Do you think you'll like that?

HATSHEPSUT: Please don't underestimate me. I've already put in the boy's application for further training with the high priests—but the boy doesn't know that he's applied. I'll make certain that he's accepted. That will take up at least six more years.

SENMUT: Six years! Now you are talking.

HATSHEPSUT: More than six years! I've got big plans to help my kingdom.

NUT: Soon Hatshepsut made sure that six years stretched into ten and ten into about twenty. Hatshepsut had plenty of time to make sure that her plans became reality.

HATSHEPSUT: Our country has been spending too much time in foreign wars. It's time that we focused on rebuilding our country. We need buildings that will inspire our people and please the gods!

HATHOR: As promised, Senmut became her master builder. He constructed monuments, tombs, and great temples carved out of rock.

NUT: But Hatshepsut wasn't satisfied.

HATSHEPSUT: Over one thousand years ago our people built the great pyramids in the desert near Giza. I want to do something that will inspire our people. I want to do something that was never done before.

SENMUT: Isn't being the first major female Pharaoh enough?

HATSHEPSUT: No, it's not enough. I want to explore the world and trade with people from far away. That will light a fire in the hearts of the people.

NUT: Therefore, Hatshepsut sent an expedition to the faraway land of Punt, a land in the distant south that was a mystery to most Egyptians.

HATHOR: It was like sending ships off the edge of the world.

NUT: But it worked.

HATHOR: After months the ships returned.

NUT: They carried some of the strangest things the Egyptians had ever seen.

SENMUT: *(standing in amazement as the ships pass by)* What on earth did they bring back?

HATSHEPSUT: I'm not sure myself, but I want all this recorded on the walls of my tomb.

HATHOR: The ships were full of ivory, ebony, and fragrant gum trees ready to be replanted in Egyptian soil.

NUT: They brought back live animals, too. Baboons scampered around the decks and hung from the riggings.

HATHOR: As the ships sailed along the Nile, the Egyptians came to the riverside and stood with their mouths open.

EGYPTIAN ONE: Look at all these things. It's as if a whole new world is passing before our eyes.

EGYPTIAN TWO: King Hatshepsut is responsible for it all.

EGYPTIAN ONE: You mean Queen Hatshepsut, I believe.

EGYPTIAN TWO: I thought that . . .

NUT: The people had some good reasons to be confused, too.

HATSHEPSUT: Senmut, did you see how those men at my last audience were disrespectful?

SENMUT: No, Your Highness, I didn't. What did they do?

HATSHEPSUT: Well, they didn't actually do anything, but they looked at me funny. I think it's because I'm a woman. They don't respect me.

SENMUT: I disagree, Your Highness. Everyone reveres you. You may not wear a beard, but . . .

HATSHEPSUT: That's it. From now on, I'll wear a beard. Give me one of those little paste-on beards that the young men wear.

SENMUT: Right away, Your Highness. Will there be anything else?

HATSHEPSUT: Yes, as a matter of fact, there is. From now on, I want all of my statues to have a beard, too.

NUT: Hatshepsut knew that most people never got a glimpse of the Pharaoh but that statues could be set up around the entire kingdom. It was clever public relations.

HATSHEPSUT: Now there will be no laughing at the "female pharaoh!"

SENMUT: Yes, Your Highness. (*to himself*) But I liked you better the way you were!

SCENE FIVE

HATHOR: Hatshepsut's reign continued, and her power grew, but so did the number of her critics.

NUT: Though many respected her, others became critical of her decisions.

EGYPTIAN ONE: Isn't it great the way that Hatshepsut has spent time and money building temples and putting people to work. They say this is what it was like in the "olden days," when everyone pitched in to build the great pyramids.

EGYPTIAN TWO: Great? Are you kidding? She may be building temples, but she's not paying any attention to the rest of the world. The Greeks don't respect us anymore. Other kingdoms are challenging us. Foreign affairs should be the number-one priority.

EGYPTIAN ONE: (*angrily*) Oh, so you know so much about politics, do you?

EGYPTIAN TWO: More than you do.

EGYPTIAN ONE: (*sarcastically*) I bet you're smater than the Pharaoh, too!

HATHOR: During this time the "real" Pharaoh, Thutmose III, was getting older and restless. Remember, Hatshepsut had made sure that he stayed in the shadows while she actually ruled the kingdom.

THUTMOSE III: *(impatiently)* All right. Enough waiting. I'm ready for my coronation now.

HIGH PRIEST: Yes, Your Highness. However, your aunt says that she'll be glad to schedule it when the stars are in the proper alignment.

THUTMOSE III: Just when will that be?

HIGH PRIEST: In about five years, by the royal astronomer's calculations.

THUTMOSE III: I think it's time for a new royal astronomer to be appointed.

HIGH PRIEST: That is impossible. The Queen has appointed this one for life.

THUTMOSE III: I was afraid of that. Of course, life can end very unexpectedly.

HIGH PRIEST: My lord, I have good news to report. The temple you wanted built in honor of Isis has been completed. It's beautiful.

THUTMOSE III: Excellent. Did you bring me a copy of the inscription, as I asked?

HIGH PRIEST: Yes, but . . . I don't want to bore you with the inscription. You know, if you've heard one dedication, you've heard them all. That is just a bit of priestly humor.

THUTMOSE III: I'm not amused. Read it or you'll be mummified sooner than you expected.

HIGH PRIEST: "In honor of Isis, the eternal, this temple has been built by the noble, reverent, all-powerful ruler of the golden land of Egypt . . ."

THUTMOSE III: I like that "all-powerful" part. Go on.

HIGH PRIEST: *(voice shaking a bit)* ". . . Hatshepsut, incarnation of the god Horus, Queen of Upper and Lower Egypt."

THUTMOSE III: *(angrily)* Hatshepsut! Hatshepsut! She put her name on my temple! Am I even mentioned?

HIGH PRIEST: Oh, yes, my lord. You are definitely named, "noble son of Thutmose II," right after a brief reference to the royal builder, Senmut.

THUTMOSE III: What? After the builder! A commoner named before me! This is the height of disrespect! I'll tolerate it no longer!

HIGH PRIEST: Hatshepsut is very powerful, and the people love her. She builds temples. She sends explorers and traders to faraway lands. It's hard to challenge that kind of popularity. How will you get the power away from her?

THUTMOSE III: I'm not sure . . . but it won't be pretty. Do I have any troops in the palace loyal to me?

HIGH PRIEST: Yes, Your Highness.

THUTMOSE III: Do any of the nobles owe me or my deceased father favors?

HIGH PRIEST: Quite a few, sir.

THUTMOSE III: Well, then, it's payback time.

SCENE SIX

NUT: Meanwhile, back at the palace, Hatshepsut and Senmut weren't worried about anything, except their own reputations.

HATSHEPSUT: (*looking at a map on the wall*) It's been a while since my last big success. Perhaps I should send another mission to Punt or some land even farther south.

SENMUT: No. People have come to take the trade missions for granted. They don't even come to the Nile to watch them push off. I think we should build another temple. I've been thinking about a big, big temple.

HATSHEPSUT: (*speaking sarcastically*) Oh, we should build another temple, should we? Don't forget who is in charge here. Even master builders can be replaced.

SENMUT: Sorry, Your Highness. I did get a little above myself.

HATSHEPSUT: Just watch it. (*hearing some noises down the hall*) Say, what's that commotion?

SENMUT: Sounds like soldiers marching.

HATSHEPSUT: Did you order soldiers to come here without my permission?

SENMUT: No, Your Highness.

HATSHEPSUT: Well, someone has, and they are disturbing me. Tell them to be quiet. Tell them to go away.

SENMUT: *(going to the hallway)* Right away. *(shouting down the hall)* Be quiet! The Queen orders it!

HATSHEPSUT: Here I am, the incarnation of a god, and I can't even hear myself think. What is going on?

SENMUT: *(sounding nervous)* There are soldiers in the palace, but they are not listening to me.

HATSHEPSUT: The nerve of them! Well, perhaps they will listen to the Queen! Be quiet! Go away! Don't you know who I am? Stop!

SOLDIER: Sorry, Your Highness, but we have our orders to escort you out of the palace.

HATSHEPSUT: Orders? Whose orders? I give the orders around here.

SOLDIER: The orders of the Pharaoh, Thutmose III. He also ordered that we keep the builder here, temporarily, of course.

HATSHEPSUT: What's happening? Senmut, what's happening to us?

SENMUT: *(sadly)* It's over, my Queen. We're history now.

HATHOR: What happened that night, no one knows. In the morning Thutmose III was sitting on the throne of Egypt.

SCENE SEVEN

NUT: After Thutmose III gained power, he did everything he could to make Egypt forget about Hatshepsut.

SOLDIER: What are your orders, Your Highness?

THUTMOSE III: I've been cheated out of twenty years of fame. Now Hatshepsut will know what it's like to be unknown. *(to soldier)* Go throughout the land. Wherever you see the name Hatshepsut, destroy it. Use chisels, axes, hammers, whatever you need.

SOLDIER: And what should I put in place of her name?

THUTMOSE III: Put my name, and the name of Thutmose II, and the great Thutmose I. Let the world think that *we* built up Egypt.

SOLDIER: What about the name of the builder, Senmut?

THUTMOSE III: *(angrily)* That commoner had the nerve to put his name before mine! I don't want a trace of his memory to exist. His name must be erased from every temple and every public building. *(getting more intense)* Go to his own tomb and destroy it.

SOLDIER: Yes, sir. Your commands will be carried out!

NUT: And so ends the story of the amazing Hatshepsut.

HATHOR: Not quite. The soldiers didn't do a thorough job.

NUT: They destroyed much of Hatshepsut's legacy, but they missed a temple near the city of Thebes. On that temple's walls, the pictures and stories of her reign survived.

HATHOR: That temple was built by her friend, Senmut.

NUT: What happened to him?

HATHOR: No one knows. It seems that Thutmose III took a special interest in destroying his memory. He's gone completely. Even his mummy was never found.

NUT: However, nothing can remained buried in the sands of Egypt forever. Just as archeologists continue to uncover the secrets of tombs sealed and hidden centuries ago, storytellers will continue to discover the story of Hatshepsut.

THE END

AFTER READING

TALK ABOUT IT

Pharaoh's Adviser
If you were an adviser to Thutmose I and he asked for advice about naming his daughter as the next ruler, what would you say? How would you suggest that he handle criticism?

Coping With Anger
Hatshepsut's mother, Ahmose, supports her daughter, but she can't change the Pharaoh's mind. Imagine a conversation between Hatshepsut and her mother. How would Ahmose deal with the girl's anger at being passed over? What practical suggestions could she make to help Hatshepsut deal with the situation?

Approach the Bench
Thutmose III thinks that he has been wronged by Hatshepsut. Imagine that he stood before a court and demanded the right to rule. What arguments would he make in his effort to convince the judge the he deserved to be pharaoh? Would he appeal to reason? To emotions?

EXTENSION ACTIVITIES

Influential People
Ask students to research the life of another woman, real or fictitious, from the ancient world. They may want to choose Cleopatra, Helen of Troy, or perhaps Dido from the *Aeneid*. What power or influence did these women hold? How did they obtain their power?

Thanks for the Memories
Hatshepsut's memoirs would make fascinating reading, but they've never been found. (*They may never have been written.*) Take one episode of Hatshepsut's life and have students write about it from her perspective. What would she be proudest of? Would she have any regrets?

Edge of the World
Sailing the wide ocean was terrifying and dangerous for ancient peoples, yet mariners found the courage to do it. What tricks did those ancient sailors use to navigate strange waters? What sorts of vessels did they have?

Leading Women poster
Make a poster of women who are leaders. Note any of the women who have campaigned for, or been elected to, a leadership position in your community, your state, and the nation.

Additional Resources

Here are several books that may prove helpful to you and your students as you continue your study of Egypt.

For Teachers

Aldred, Cyril. *The Egyptians.* New York: Thames and Hudson Inc., 1984.

Erman, Adolph. *Ancient Egyptian Poetry and Prose.* New York: Dover Publications, 1995.

Erman, Adolph. *Life in Ancient Egypt.* New York: Dover Publications, 1971.

Green, Roger. *Tales of Ancient Egypt.* New York: Penguin Books, 1979.

Hart, George. *Egyptian Myths.* Texas: University of Texas Press, 1995.

Herodotus. *The History.* Chicago: University of Chicago Press, 1987.

Spence, Lewis. *Ancient Egyptian Myths and Legend.* New York: Dover Publications, 1990.

For Students

David, Rosalie. *Handbook to Life in Ancient Egypt.* New York: Facts on File, 1998.

Ferguson, Sheila. *Growing Up in Ancient Egypt.* United Kingdom: Anchor Brendon Ltd., 1980.

Halliwell, Sarah, ed. *Gods and Pharoahs of Ancient Egypt.* New Jersey: Chartwell Books, 1998.

Macaulay, David. *Pyramid.* New York: Houghton Mifflin Company, 1975.

Mann, Elizabeth. *The Great Pyramid.* New York: Mikaya Press, 1996.